More Praise for *Li*

"Listening to a sermon is a spiritual discipline—that is the simple, profound insight that underpins this rich offering from Will Willimon. It's an insight that could—indeed, should—reshape the homiletical experience of both preachers and congregants (or, to use the more old-fashioned but also more apt term, auditors). I know that it has already begun reshaping mine."
—Lauren F. Winner, Associate Professor, Duke Divinity School, Durham, NC

"Though he's written numerous books on the art of preaching, no one can preach like the inestimable Will Willimon. But everyone can learn to do the holy work of listening to any sermon more deeply, actively, and responsively with the help of Will's insightful and enjoyable guidance in this book. As Jesus said, 'Whoever has ears to listen should pay attention!' Now perhaps we can."
—Peter M. Wallace, author, Episcopal priest, and host of "Day1" weekly sermon podcast

"Books about preaching—how to research, write, and deliver sermons—are legion. But books about how sermons are heard, internalized, and acted upon by ordinary Christians in the pews are rare. Drawing on decades of experience as a parish minister, university chaplain, divinity school faculty member, and United Methodist bishop of distinction, Willimon addresses this elusive yet critically important task with his usual wit, acumen, and pastor's heart. A few hours pondering this thought-filled work will pay handsome dividends come Sunday."
—Grant Wacker, Gilbert T. Rowe Distinguished Professor of Christian History, Duke Divinity School, Durham, NC

"There is no shortage of resources out there for how to prepare and preach a sermon, and yet faith comes from hearing. In turning our attention to the homiletical process of listening, Willimon has given clergy and laity alike a true gift. Together, we get to listen for God's daring Word—a word that in our hearing brings about holy obedience, persistent hope, and daring discipleship."

—Karoline M. Lewis, Marbury E. Anderson Chair of Biblical Preaching, Professor of Biblical Preaching, Luther Seminary; Program Director, Festival of Homiletics

"Interweaving a half century of experiences and a library of knowledge of the biblical text, theology, and preaching, Will Willimon challenges preachers and audiences alike to listen to God's powerful Word. Written in his inimitable style and from deep faith, this is a book that will make you laugh, think, and remember. It deserves reading by all who participate in the common but strange world of a sermon."

—Gregory E. Sterling, The Reverend Henry L. Slack Dean, Lillian Claus Professor of New Testament, Yale Divinity School, New Haven, CT

Other Abingdon Press Books by Will Willimon

Preachers Dare

Stories by Willimon

Will Willimon's Lectionary Sermon Resources Series

Fear of the Other

Who Lynched Willie Earle?

Pastor, Revised Edition

Holy Spirit (with Stanley Hauerwas)

Resident Aliens (with Stanley Hauerwas)

Incarnation

Sinning Like a Christian

Why Jesus?

This We Believe

WILL WILLIMON

LISTENERS DARE

Hearing God in the Sermon

Abingdon Press
Nashville

LISTENERS DARE:
Hearing God in the Sermon

Copyright © 2022 by William H. Willimon

ISBN: 978-1-7910-2398-0

Library of Congress Control Number: 2022933637

22 23 24 25 26 27 28 29 30 31—10 9 8 7 6 5 4 3 2 1
MANUFACTURED IN THE UNITED STATES OF AMERICA

Happy are your ears because they hear. I assure you that many prophets and righteous people wanted to see what you see and hear what you hear, but they didn't.
—Matt 13:15-17

CONTENTS

Contents

6. Responding to the Sermon 87
When have you heard a sermon that moved you to action?
How have sermons equipped you to be a "doer of the word"?

7. Hearing Aid 97
How could you help your pastor be a more effective preacher?
How might you better prepare to hear God speak to you
through a sermon?

INTRODUCTION

Here's my celebration of my fiftieth anniversary of working with a God who (unlike other gods) dares to speak (even from a burning bush) to folk who (like Moses), even though they (like I) had not asked God to speak, dared (like you and I) to listen anyway.

"Reveal yourself!" we cried to God down through the ages. God spoke Jesus, The Word tenting among us (John 1:1). Jesus's main occupation? Jesus came preaching (Mark 1:14).

The gospel is news that passes from the lips of one who has heard to the ears of one who may not yet have heard, then (God willing) burrows into the soul, energizing heart and hands in daring response to news received. Preaching is instigated by an astounding claim: *Good news: God has spoken to us.* The Christian life is what you get when ordinary folk respond: *Keep talking, I'm all ears.*

At least sixty-five million Americans (20.4 percent of us) heard a sermon last week.[1] Any preacher who complains that listeners are oblivious to sermons must reckon with the survey that showed that for 83 percent of Christians, the sermon is the top reason for choosing and staying in a congregation.[2]

Listeners are more interesting than we who preach to them. I open my class at Duke by showing students "The Preaching of Saint John the Baptist," by Pieter Bruegel the Elder. A throng of sixteenth-century Flemish people congregate in the woods. A Dutch town with its church stands at a distance. See? Here, in

Holland, it's Luke 3:1-18 all over again. Bruegel has done what preachers do most every Sunday—take an ancient biblical story, plop it into our place and time, saying "Speak!"

"The Preaching of Saint John the Baptist," Pieter Bruegel

You wouldn't know it's a depiction of a preacher at work had I not told you. There is no single focal point. Listeners—some attentive, many distracted, looking down from perches in trees or gawking up while squatting on the ground, in animated conversation, gossiping, buying and selling, showing off their purchases, gambling, flirting with one another, or posing in their fine clothing—jam-pack the painting.

"Listeners—A Few Listening, Many Not—to a Sermon by John the Baptist" would be a more telling title.

It takes some searching to find the preacher—unarmed, undistinguished, oddly and insignificantly dressed, gesturing, confronting, connecting with the crowd with nothing but words.

How right of the painter to spotlight the listeners rather than the speaker. It's not a sermon until it's heard. Listeners crowd around and push into a sermon, focus or ignore, climb up to it or look down upon it, perk up their ears, or willfully, dumbly gaze out into the world, thinking thoughts other than those the preacher begs them to think. Rather than listen to the preacher, many intended hearers continue their worldly conversation, barely eavesdropping upon the preacher's words. Distractions are manifold.

Detail of St. John the Baptist

And yet, for all the reasons why people fail to listen, much less to hear, Luke says multitudes braved the discomforting wilderness and dared venture out to listen to John preach, hoping for news they couldn't hear any other way, yearning for a good sermon as if their lives depended upon it.

What does it say about me as a preacher that when I look at Bruegel's painting I focus on those who're not listening rather than on the hopeful, upturned faces of those who—despite all the perfectly good reasons they shouldn't—listen?

Even King Herod—nasty piece of work though he was— "respected John" and "regarded him as a righteous and holy person." While "John's words greatly confused Herod," something about John's preaching made the king enjoy "listening to him" (Mark 6:20). God only knows why Herod listened to John's sermons even though he was clueless as to their meaning. (Preachers note: Herod's adoration of John's incomprehensible sermons didn't deter Herod from serving up John's head on a platter.)

Preachers Dare: Speaking for God was based on my Yale lectures on preaching.[3] No sooner had I finished than I realized that in my attempt to encourage fellow preachers I had neglected you listeners. Though God must give us preachers chutzpa and courage, a speech isn't a sermon until God produces you daring hearers. News, particularly gospel Good News, is meant to be heard as good news for all. The world is quite right in judging the Christian faith by its exemplification in the lives of its hearers. Or as Jesus put it, "Happy rather are those who hear God's word and put it into practice" (Luke 11:28).

In his classic *How to Read a Book*, philosopher Mortimer Adler said, "Theoretic books teach you that something is the case. Practical books teach you how to do something which you should do."[4] This book attempts a bit of both. However, be warned: this can't be a do-it-yourself handbook on "How to listen to a sermon" because hearing—really hearing—a sermon occurs only with miraculous divine aid. Just like Moses standing before a bush that speaks, you can't tell God's word to yourself.

My hope is to help preachers to deliver the news about Christ and to enable all listeners—clergy and lay—to dare to get more out of sermons in light of Christ's daring determination to get more out of us.[5]

Will Willimon

GOD IN CONVERSATION

The word is near you, in your mouth and in your heart (that is, the message of faith that we preach). . . . The scripture says, All who have faith in him won't be put to shame. . . . All who call on the Lord's name will be saved. So how can they call on someone they don't have faith in? And how can they have faith in someone they haven't heard of? And how can they hear without a preacher? . . . So, faith comes from listening, but it's listening by means of Christ's message. But I ask you, didn't they hear it? Definitely! Their voice has gone out into the entire earth, and their message has gone out to the corners of the inhabited world. . . . And Isaiah even dares to say, I was found by those who didn't look for me; I revealed myself to those who didn't ask for me.
(Rom 10:8, 11, 13, 15, 17-20)

Faith comes from listening (Rom 10:17). A Christian is somebody who has dared listen to and then live the Good News. The major difference between a Christian and a not-yet-Christian? The Christian has received news the non-Christian has yet to hear.

We are as we hear. "Tell me who you listen to for your daily news," said the pollster, "and I can predict your stand on a dozen issues."

Acoustically generated, Christianity is training in empty-handed receptivity. "We have heard it, God, with our own ears; our ancestors told us about it: about the deeds you did in their

1

days, in days long past" (Ps 44:1). Nobody is born knowing either chemistry or Christ. Want to be a chemist? Find somebody to speak the mysteries of the periodic table until you hear and assimilate what you've heard. Teachers of chemistry must hand over their stuff with skill, but receivers also bear responsibility to be receptive to the truths of chemistry, submitting to the practices of chemists, internalizing the moves. To claim with credibility, "I'm a chemist" is also to say, "I've been a good listener."

So it is with Christianity: hearing of the faith precedes believing and performing the faith.

Not sure what to think about Jesus? Don't worry. He makes relationship with you his self-assignment, loves to talk, can't be shut up, even by a crucifixion, and promises in the end to have his say. The last word on your status with God is his. Your best hope is that he'll keep talking, refusing to be stumped by lousy listening.

That sermon is "good," which spurs performance as listeners become hearers who turn out to be actors. In all times and places, notwithstanding the many impediments for reception of the gospel, millions have shamelessly stepped on stage and assumed their role in Christ's drama of salvation, with no other justification for their risky performance than the news they have heard.

Jesus took preaching as his main job, then turned around and made proclamation the vocation of all disciples (Matt 10:5-7), commanding us to tell the world news that the world can't tell itself. Sometimes with a self-effacing whisper, occasionally with a defiant, exuberant shout (Matt 10:27), all Christians must hand over what we've heard. "Tell the next generation all about the praise due the Lord and his strength—the wondrous works God has done" (Ps 78:4). "You are witnesses of these things," Christ preaching to you so that you'll be a witness who proclaims Christ to others (1 John 1:1-3), speaking out, acting up in Jesus's name when God gives you the chance.

Somebody at work says, "You're an intelligent person, so how can you fall for all that Jesus stuff?" Or, "I used to go to church every now and again, but then I realized that the church is full of homophobic, racist people, and I just don't believe in that."

You buy time saying, "I'd like to hear more," as you pray, *Lord, thanks for the thousand sermons I've sat through that prepared me for this moment.*

Don't want to be a preacher? Jesus doesn't care; all who sign on with Jesus are commissioned to speak the news they have received to others who've heard and to those who haven't. Sorry, if that wasn't made clear at your baptism.

Though we preachers love to blame our failures upon our lousy listeners, truth to tell, many listeners report frustration at their preacher's failure to help them move from listening to hearing, really hearing, and then doing the Word. Listeners help God craft better preachers.

He owned a hardware store. . . . Someone had warned me about him when I moved there. "He's usually quiet," they said, "but be careful." People still recalled the Sunday in 1970 when, in the middle of the sermon (the previous preacher's weekly diatribe against Nixon and the Vietnam War), he had stood up from where he was sitting, shook his head, and walked right out. So, I always preached with one eye on my notes and the other on him. He hadn't walked out on a sermon in years. Still, a preacher can never be too safe.

You can imagine my fear when one Sunday, having waited until everyone had shaken my hand and left the narthex, he approached me, gritting his teeth and muttering, "I just don't see things your way, preacher."

I moved into my best mode of non-defensive defensiveness, assuring him that my sermon was just one way of looking at things, and that perhaps he had misinterpreted what I said, and even if he had not, I could very well be wrong and er, uh . . .

"Don't you back off with me," he snapped. "I just said that your sermon shook me up. I didn't ask you to take it back. Stick by your guns—if you're a real preacher."

Then he said to me, with an almost desperate tone, "Preacher, I run a hardware store. Since you've never had a real job, let me explain it to you. Now, you can learn to run a hardware store in about six months. I've been there *fifteen years.* That means that all week, nobody talks to me like I know anything. I'm not like you, don't get to sit around and read books and talk about important things. It's just me and that hardware store. Sunday morning and your sermons are all I've got. Please, don't you dare take it back."[1]

Good preachers must have well-tuned ears; we're able to preach only what we have been enabled to hear. Just like you listeners, preachers are Christian on the basis of news we have heard. Discipleship is not self-sustainable; only through doggedly persistent, patient, prolonged, Sunday-after-Sunday listening do any of us stay Christian.

That's why this book is for both preachers and listeners, listeners all.

And God Said

According to my reading of Genesis, God created humanity because God loves conversation.[2] Everything begins with something said and then heard. Before time and creation, God— Father, Son, and Holy Spirit—were one in constant, harmonious colloquy, one God in three ways of continual, conversational communion. The genesis of the world is a sermon God preached to the formless, silent void, "Let there be light" (Gen 1:3). All God needed to do was say "Light," and there was light. God's word is performative; God says the word and creation is as good as done (Ps 33:9).

Humanity is generated by majestic, sovereign speech: "Let there be people . . ." and there were. The conversation that is the rest of scripture suggests to me that "created in the image of God" (Gen 1:27) means we were made for listening, hearing, and responding to a God who loves to talk.

Before the first humanoids got around to gardening or procreation, they engaged in conversation (Gen 3:1-7). Alas, speaking and hearing as gifts of God can also be means for rebellion against God. The snake interlocutor wants to talk theology, raising questions like: "Are you sure you heard God say . . . ?"

The man and woman repeat what they heard. The snake tells them that they heard wrong (Gen 3:4). The result of this skeptical conversation? They saw, desired, took, and ate the forbidden fruit (Gen 3:6). Shortly thereafter, when bad turned to worse, people began to call upon God (Gen 4:26), but not before God called us out, telling us tough truths we would never have told ourselves (Gen. 3:13-19). Through words, we met the God we could not have found on our own.

That's the God of Israel and the church for you, addressing us before we talk to God, refusing to allow us to determine the limits of divine-human communication, rejecting our attempts to hear only what we want, God willing to talk to rebellious listeners who push back, distort, and doubt what they hear.

While there's much we don't know about God, we do know this from scripture: God prefers colloquy to soliloquy, thank God. Millions have tried to shut their ears to God and have failed, so determined is God to draw all into conversation. Though we often complain of hearing too little from God, there's a good chance that over a lifetime of listening to sermons, God will tell you more than you'll ever be able to handle.

Thus, in speaking about his own preaching, Paul wrote: "For God, who said, 'Let light shine out of darkness,' made his light shine in our hearts to give us the light of the knowledge of God's glory displayed in the face of Christ" (2 Cor 4:6). Get it? Whenever a preacher is heard, it's light-out-of-darkness new creation all over again, this time in someone's life.

Listening for the God Who Listens

Atop the Mount of Transfiguration, Peter exclaimed, "Let's get busy and build three booths each for Jesus, Elijah, and Moses." Let's set up permanent housing for this mysterious vision. No. The heavenly voice told Peter to shut up and listen (Matt 17:5). If Jesus is indeed the "beloved Son" should we build a substantial, protective encasement for him? No. "Listen to him."[3]

Take the Transfiguration as a parable of what it means to be the church.

As challenging as preaching can be, you listeners have your hands full, daring a transfiguring Jesus to give you an ear full. What does God expect? "Listen" and after daunting listening, dare to go back down the mountain and tell what we've heard:

> Israel, listen! Our God is the Lord! Only the Lord! Love the Lord your God with all your heart, all your being, and all your strength. These words that I am commanding you today must always be on your minds. Recite them to your children. Talk about them when you are sitting around your house and when you are out and about, when you are lying down and when you are getting up. Tie them on your hand as a sign. They should be on your forehead as a symbol.

Write them on your house's doorframes and on your city's gates.
(Deut 6:4-8)

In the Bible, the "ear" is synonymous with the "heart" or the "mind" as the organ of cognition and understanding (Prov 2:2). While human hearing is a gift of God (Ps 94:9; Prov 20:12), God's listening is among God's greatest gifts (Pss 18:6; 40:1). "The one who made the ear, can't he hear?" (Ps 94:9). A fake god (aka, "idol") has no ear for prayer (Deut 4:28; Pss 115:6; 135:17). Much biblical supplication begins with a plea to God to listen (2 Kgs 19:16; Neh 1:6; Ps 5:1). Such pleas are unnecessary; God's hearing is so sharp that God hears even before we speak (Ps 139:4).

God's ears are always open to the cries of the righteous and the needy (Pss 10:17-18; 34:15). Hearing the groans of the enslaved, God initiates the Exodus (Exod 2:24; 3:7). Needy ones ask on the presumption that they'll be heard (1 John 5:14).

God is such a good listener that God's ears are not solely attuned to Israel. At the dedication of the temple in Jerusalem, Solomon prays: "Listen also to the immigrant who isn't from your people Israel but who comes from a distant country" so that "they will hear of your great reputation, your great power, and your outstretched arm." The immigrant who hears will come to the temple, speak to Israel's God and then God will "listen from heaven . . . and do everything the immigrant asks" (1 Kgs 8:41-43).

Still, God is free not to hear. Sometimes human sin hinders God's hearing (Isa 59:1-2; Job 27:8-9; 35:12-13). Human refusal to hear the cries of the needy results in God's refusal to hear prayer (Prov 21:13). God turned a deaf ear to Jeremiah's prayer on behalf of sinful Israel (Jer 7:16; 14:11-12). God hears, but not at our command. Job complains for thirty-eight chapters before there's any indication that God is listening; God hears, but not always on our schedule.

When one of his disciples whips out a sword—stand your ground, self-defense in action—and severs the ear of one of those arresting Jesus, Jesus rebukes him and restores his enemy's hearing (Luke 22:50-51). I heard a great sermon by Dr. James Forbes on that text: we use our swords to silence others whereas God wants all, especially those who would harm God, to hear.

The command, "Israel listen!" (Deut 6:4), precedes many prophetic pronouncements. Whereas God could command us to work or to fight, God asks us to listen. "Hear the Lord" is repeated thirty times among the prophets, more often than "obey" or "do."

Each generation must listen carefully so that it can speak to the young about the Lord's goodness (Pss 44:1; 78:3-4). God's people are to attend to the reading of the sacred texts (Deut 31:1-12; Neh 8:3; Rev 1:3). A "child of God" is someone who hears the words of God (John 8:47). The sheep of God's pasture hear the voice of the Shepherd (John 10:3, 16, 27). Our first duty to God? *Listen.*

Lack of hearing is occasionally attributed to divine judgment upon human sin, as in Isaiah 6:10 or Deuteronomy 29:4. Amos predicts there'll be a day when there's a famine in the land, not of bread but of "hearing the Lord's words" (Amos 8:11). Yet the day will come when God shall restore Israel's auditory ability (Isa 32:3).

Sometimes listeners hear God speaking distinctly, as when God called to Moses from the burning bush, gave Moses the Ten Commandments (Deut 5:22; Isa 6:8), or ordered Peter directly to let go of his prejudices and receive even the Gentiles for baptism (Acts 10:13). God's word is spoken straightforwardly into the prophet's ears and then passed to the people so that listening to a prophet is hearing straight from God (Isa 22:14; Ezek 3:10-11, 17; Deut 18:19). Harriet Tubman read Exodus and thought it was talking about her and her enslaved people. Tubman's nickname? Moses.

The Israelites, in terror at the thought of actually hearing God, ask Moses, "You go and listen to all that the LORD our God says. Then tell us all that the LORD our God speaks to you. We'll listen and we'll do it" (Deut 5:27). Moses's intermediary prophetic role will be reprised next Sunday when your preacher rises to preach, though unaccompanied by a gutsy congregational pledge to listen and to do.

Elijah expected to hear God in wind, earthquake, and fire but heard nothing. Only after a "Thin. Quiet" did the prophet hear (1 Kgs 19:11-12). God's word is often subtle, gentle, like falling snow or rain (Isa 55:10). When Jesus, deeply troubled, cried out to the Father, there was a sound from heaven. Three out of five listeners said, "It's thunder," but the rest thought, "An angel spoke to him." None recognized the voice of God (John 12:27-29). In my experience, rarely is God's word obvious.

Disciples are blessed because they have heard the message of the coming kingdom that God's people have longed to hear (Matt 13:16-17). Jesus repeatedly urges those who hear to act upon what he says (Mark 4:9, 23, etc.). The heavenly voice of Revelation says that listening is the key to understanding what God is up to in God's climactic restoration of creation (Rev 2:7, 11, etc.). Christ promises that even the dead will "hear the voice of the son of God" and come to life (John 5:25). "Untie him and let him go" shouts Jesus, and his once-dead friend Lazarus strides forth from the tomb (John 11:1-44).

Though God is unheeded by rulers of the world (1 Cor 2:6), the lowly and foolish hear good news.

Listen!

There may be faiths that arise from your sweet subjectivity, accompany your birth, secluded meditation, silent walks in the woods, discoveries from human experience (good and bad), or what you've learned from licking your wounds. Christianity isn't one of them.

> "Listen to this! A farmer went out to scatter seed. As he was scattering seed, some fell on the path; and the birds came and ate it. Other seed fell on rocky ground where the soil was shallow. They sprouted immediately because the soil wasn't deep. When the sun came up, it scorched the plants; and they dried up because they had no roots. Other seed fell among thorny plants. The thorny plants grew and choked the seeds, and they produced nothing. Other seed fell into good soil and bore fruit. Upon growing and increasing, the seed produced in one case a yield of thirty to one, in another case a yield of sixty to one, and in another case a yield of one hundred to one." He said, "Whoever has ears to listen should pay attention!" (Mark 4:3-9)

Listen to this! Nobody is born believing that God is a Jew from Nazareth who lived briefly, died violently, rose unexpectedly, and resumed speaking to those who betrayed him. Somebody must give us words that open doors into the faith called Christianity. All we must do is listen. Without submitting to God's address, we're unable to love without first being loved, incapable of discovering without being found, inept to speak to without being addressed. Through conversation, God gets through to us. While we were struggling to get our minds around God, surprise: God already had us in mind. Striving to be spiritual—to heft ourselves out of hemmed-in humanity—God turned toward us, asking, "Where are you?" (Gen 3:9).[4]

A farmer went out to scatter seed. Divine/human conversation is at God's instigation, God's initiative, that is, grace: unmerited, unearned, the gift of testimony of the saints both living and dead, a God-breathed ancient book that speaks today, a Sunday sermon that the Holy Spirit commandeered to speak to you especially.

Other seed fell on rocky ground where the soil was shallow. Hearing what God says is not self-determined. We are subject to a cacophony of voices. Every sermon, even the most eloquent, risks refusal. Incomprehension is ubiquitous.

Other seed fell into good soil and bore fruit. Still, we do hear. Only God talks us into God and, surprise, in Jesus Christ, God does. The God afforded in scripture is loquacious, lavish, a revealing, determined conversationalist who revels not only in being God but also in telling us all about it. God's word is fruitful; God helps us hear.

Whoever has ears to listen should pay attention!

The church dares to be attentive to the God who is determined to be in conversation with us, the God we would never have made up for ourselves, the God who is known nonviolently, primarily through hearing the good news that God has turned toward us.

Through the ages we asked, "Is God really with us or not?" (Exod 17:1-7). In response, God comes alongside us through words: the Word Made Flesh; Moses called to by a talking bush; Mary announcing the beginning of God's revolution through a song (Luke 1:46-55); the preacher John the Baptist, precursor to John's cousin; the paradigmatic preacher, Jesus.

Sermon listeners regularly reenact this odd, old story: Moses has murdered a man back in Egypt. He's not thinking about conversation with God; he's on the lam in Midian, keeping his head down, working for his pagan priest father-in-law (Exod 3:1-12).

Moses evaded his Egyptian pursuers, but not the Lord. On Mount Horeb, Moses is astounded—a bush bursts into flame!

"Moses said to himself, 'Let me check out this amazing sight and find out why the bush isn't burning up.'"

The bush speaks! "God called to him out of the bush, 'Moses, Moses!'

"Moses said, 'I'm here'" (Exod 3:3-4).

The God of Moses's ancestors—with whom Israel had fallen out of conversation for centuries—has heard the cry of the enslaved and has come to deliver the Hebrews. And guess who'll help God do that?

> "So get going. I'm sending you to Pharaoh to bring my people, the Israelites, out of Egypt."
> But Moses said to God, "Who am I to go to Pharaoh and to bring the Israelites out of Egypt?" (Exod 3:10-12).

"Get going."

Moses won't have to come up with sermons on his own: "I will be with you," says the God whom Moses hears. Still, Pharaoh reacts with hardened heart to Moses's preaching (Exod 8:15, 32). Hearing from then speaking up for God is no guarantee of listener assent.

The story of Moses and the talking bush is a story of anybody who dares to listen, and in listening hears, and after hearing steps forth (albeit kicking and screaming in Moses's case), serving God on the basis of what has been heard. Daring divine speaking and intrepid human listening are at the heart of the faith of Israel and of the church. Luke says Jesus's first assault upon the world-as-it-is was from a synagogue pulpit, quoting his favorite preacher,

Isaiah: "The Spirit of the Lord is upon me . . . to preach good news" (Luke 4:18). Revolution, regime change initiated by words. Spoiler alert: though the Nazareth congregation responded with "Let's kill him," Jesus kept preaching. Still does.

Jesus came preaching. Announcing the whole truth and nothing but the truth about who God is and what God is up to, a declaration of independence from the old world and an invitation to citizenship in the new, a call to repent, to be rehabilitated, born again, and join the revolution named Jesus, God Saves (Luke 1:31).

Christian preaching is the peculiar public speaking that is evoked by the nature of the God who creates a world just by saying the word and by a Savior who never retires from speaking a new world into being. Jesus preached, commanded his followers to preach, and throughout the ages uniquely, decisively reveals himself through preaching. The God who became human flesh continues to be bodily present among us through the words of frail, finite, utterly human envoys entrusted with "the message of reconciliation" (1 Cor 5:19). These preachers speak about Jesus to frail, finite, utterly human listeners. Though their preacher is no Sojourner Truth or Billy Graham, God is so intent on conversation that some listeners hear anyhow.

Listening to Good News

To make hearing possible, our brains refuse most of the sound that enters our ears, discriminating, allowing our minds to go to work only after filtering out what the brain considers to be inconsequential. Trouble is, what our brains discard as unimportant could be just what we've been dying to hear.

Hourly we are bombarded with news. Much that passes for news is just advertising: good news! Buy this, wear that, smear this on your face and thereby get your best life now. Or most is just mere information: The Yankees won the World Series. The President has fled to Camp David for the weekend. Data we file away or else discard as soon as we've heard it.

But other news engages, makes a claim, and anticipates response. When someone shouts "Fire!" it's more than information. It's persuasive, demanding, and imperative truth. The gospel—Greek, *euangellion*, good news—is not just reported and received but is news that begs a reaction. Say to a group of famished children, "Hey, I've got bread enough for everybody!" or to the incarcerated, "Here's how to get out of jail," and you'll get a hearing.

If you've got news that could save someone's life, you'd be cold-hearted to keep it to yourself or to mumble so that the message is inaudible. A good, life-changing, world-naming message creates messengers and finds its intended audience, though you may be shocked by God's choice of both messenger and hearer.[5]

Thus, when I asked a young woman in one of my early congregations, "Carolyn, what possessed you to drop out of college—with your 3.0 GPA—and barge off to be a nurse in a clinic in Honduras?" She answered: "Because of what I heard you say in your sermon last Sunday. That bit about 'most of us are living just for ourselves.'"

Look, Carolyn, I was just preaching.

How was I—frail, fallen, finite preacher—to know that I would be the medium whereby someone heard a disruptive summons from God Almighty?

I was about to say that the trouble starts, in most Christians' lives, when somebody like me stands up, reads from scripture, and then dares to preach, "Thus sayeth the Lord . . ." No, holy discombobulation begins when someone like you dares to listen for God.

You become the young Isaiah:

> Then I heard the Lord's voice saying, "Whom should I send, and who will go for us?"
> I said, "I'm here; send me." (Isa 6:8)

Your active response to sermons is Genesis 1 all over again, a new world created out of nothing on the basis of God just saying the Word through a preacher. The dying-and-rising event at the heart of the gospel is recapitulated in you. So, when a student emerged after an Easter service in Duke Chapel saying, "I get it! It's all come together," I responded, "So, the women who ran from the tomb told the truth; he's loose!" (see Luke 24:10). The risen Christ, first day of his resurrected life, seeking out those who betrayed and deserted him in order to resume the conversation, one more time.

"The time is coming—and is here!—when the dead will hear the voice of God's Son, and those who hear it will live . . . the time is coming when all who are in their graves will hear his voice" (John 5:25, 28). Somebody—dead or living—unbound, crawls out of some tomb and says after a sermon, "I heard . . . ," a reprise of Christ's resurrection.

Dietrich Bonhoeffer spoke up for the church against the Nazis and paid dearly for it. Yet Bonhoeffer urged his seminarians in exile first to be listeners: "Our love for God begins with listening to God's Word, . . . God's love for us is shown by the fact that God not only gives us God's Word, but also lends us God's ear."

Chiding us preachers for thinking that we must always have something to say, Bonhoeffer says:

> Listening can be a greater service than speaking. Many people seek a sympathetic ear and do not find it among Christians, because these Christians are talking even when they should be listening. But Christians who can no longer listen to one another will soon no longer be listening to God either; they will always be talking even in the presence of God . . . Christians have forgotten that the ministry of listening has been entrusted to them by the one who is indeed the greater listener.[6]

Christians, "be quick to listen, slow to speak . . ." (Jas 1:19).

Listening for God in a Sermon

The greatest challenge to the aural capacities of both preachers and laity is the Trinity. God—Father, Son, and Holy Spirit—makes unique demands upon those who would dare divine-human conversation. After listening to Jesus, one day John says, "Many of his disciples who heard him said, 'This message is harsh. Who can hear it?'" (John 6:60). To their grumbling, Jesus replied: "Does this offend you?"

In the face of listeners' complaints about the sermon's abrasiveness, Jesus replied: "None can come to me unless the Father enables them to do so" (John 6:44). After this conversation on the limits of listeners' comprehension without divine help, "many of his disciples turned away and no longer accompanied him" (John 6:60-61, 65-66). Jesus wants us to hear, yes, but what Jesus wants us to hear can be hard to hear because it's true, whereas we eagerly lap up the lies we love.

"Does this offend you?" (John 6:61). Well, yes, sometimes. And yet, there you'll be next Sunday, still daring to be part of the Jesus-Church conversation in spite of Jesus's frequent offense.

When Jesus preached his very first sermon in Capernaum, demons were unleashed: "Get out of here, Jesus! Why are you messing with us? I know you!" (Mark 1:24, paraphrased). Curious. The demon knew Jesus, whereas the congregation didn't. The preacher in me wonders if the test of a sermon as God's Word is the degree of demonic resistance that it elicits.

Not all refusals of a sermon are due to sorry preaching. "The light came into the world, and people loved darkness more than the light" (John 3:19). Anybody who dares to preach with Jesus must not chicken out from declaring, "Listen up! Here's truth that you have spent all week avoiding." If listeners reject what we preach, let it not be because of our jargon-ridden speech, our corny attempts at forced colloquial comradery, or our distasteful personalities; let their rejection be due to Jesus.

Still, Jesus promised his preacher-in-training disciples, "Whoever listens to you, listens to me" (Luke 10:16). What preacher doesn't get the shakes hearing Jesus say that? And yet, Jesus said it, and after five decades of preaching, most Sundays, I believe it.

Note that Jesus didn't say, "Whoever preaches correct doctrine, preaches for me," though maybe that's implied. In declaring, "Whoever listens to you, listens to me," Jesus wasn't puffing up preachers. His stress was upon you, the listener. In preaching, God enables even untalented listeners, addressed by maladroit preachers, to listen to God.

Go ahead. Live dangerously. Throw caution to the wind. Listen.

Chapter 2

WHAT'S A SERMON FOR?

After John was arrested, Jesus came into Galilee announcing God's good news, saying, "Now is the time! Here comes God's kingdom! Change your hearts and lives, and trust this good news!" (Mark 1:14-15)

"This is the silliest thing I've ever seen!" I scoffed at my first exposure to Australian Rules Football.

"Like to hear more about the purpose of the game?" asked my Aussie host as he munched on a meat pie. "Perhaps that would put you in a better position to judge the sport."

Right. A five-minute lecture on Australian Football and my eyes were opened to a quite wonderful pastime.

If you want to hear a sermon, it's good to know what preaching is for. When you hear, "The western part of the state will continue dry and sunny," here comes a weather report. Nobody asks, "How should I deal with a difficult family situation?" after the speaker intones, "My fellow Americans, tonight I want to speak with you about . . ." Whoever complained, "You didn't tell me how I can I have a more fulfilling life?" to a speech that begins, "This month's sales figures, when compared with last month's, show that . . ."?

Preachers are listeners who speak what they've heard (2 Cor 4:13). The only way we learn how to preach is by becoming critical listeners. As Augustine noted, just as infants learn to speak by overhearing adult speakers, preachers learn through apprenticeship, listening "to eloquent speaking" rather than "pouring over the rules for eloquence."[1]

Before I'm a preacher, I'm a hearer, someone who, just like Moses, heard my name called and said, "I don't know where you will take me, but nevertheless, I will go. Hope you know what you are doing. Go ahead, tell me what you want your people to hear and give me the guts to say it."

A sermon is a guided, public conversation in which a preacher (1) rises up in the middle of the conversation between God and God's people, (2) speaks with God to the church, and then (3) listens for the response by the church to what has been heard.

Though preaching isn't the safest way to make a living, you listeners have got your work cut out for you in trying to hear God in a sermon:

- A "good" sermon is measured by criteria that don't apply to other public speaking.

- Listeners have not been privy to what preachers have been up to in preparing a sermon.

- Preachers speak about, to, and for God; who God is and what God says greatly complicate the listeners' task.

It's a heck of a way for God to obtain what God wants, this archaic practice called preaching, still it's uniquely God's way: "In God's wisdom, he determined that the world wouldn't come to know him through its wisdom. Instead, God was pleased to save those who believe through the foolishness of preaching" (1 Cor 1:21).

Active Listening

I once suffered an administrator who announced, "My administration will begin with conversations with each of you faculty." Somebody had told her that good leaders are good listeners.

Upon entering her office, I was greeted with, "Take a seat. I want to hear what you have to say."

I responded, "Er, uh, well, uh, what is it you'd like to know?"

"Whatever you want to tell me."

Nervously, I began a rambling, incoherent monologue about my family, my research interests, our new dog, and Duke's basketball prospects. The administrator stared at me blankly. After an eternal twenty minutes, she looked at her watch and sighed, "I'm glad we had this conversation."

I awkwardly rose, mumbled, and left with no reason to believe that I had shared anything with anyone much less had a "conversation."

Few experiences are more painful, especially for a garrulous person like me, than to talk to (rather than with) someone who sits passively, unresponsively, as I drone on. Who knows if they're listening, but it's sure that they aren't hearing.

Preaching as monologue—I talk, you sit quietly and listen—is deadly. I hand you a package. You accept it without opening. Sermon DOA.

That's why most preachers prefer to receive even angry hostility from a few hearers rather than widespread blank stares; at least we've been heard. No matter how well collected and ordered a preacher's thoughts are on paper, it's not a sermon if it's not intended for and received by somebody.

Tom Long portrays listeners' active participation in the production of a sermon:

> The hearer is not at all passive in the listing process. The space between pulpit and pew bristles with energy and activity. As the preacher speaks, the hearer races ahead in anticipation of what might be said next, ranges back over what has already been said, debates with the preacher, rearranges the material, wanders away and returns (sometimes!). In short, the hearer is a co-creator of the sermon. Preachers may be passing out eggs, but hearers are making omelets and a sermon preached to 75 people will be transformed by them into 75 more-or-less related sermons.[2]

What's a Good Sermon?

Bet you have in mind how a "good sermon" sounds, even though you've not had the nerve to share your criteria with your preacher. What's a sermon for? Try this:

> A sermon is "good" when God chooses to reveal to God's people through a preacher what God has to say and enables listeners to hear and faithfully respond to what they've heard.

To help you ask the right questions of a sermon so that you can better hear a sermon, I'll let you listeners in on some professional secrets. Here's what I, as a homiletician (a preaching professor), tell my seminarians (would-be preachers) about how to deliver a "good" sermon.

A Good Sermon

The Purpose of Preaching

The biblical preacher, in service to the congregation, goes to the biblical text, hoping to make a discovery. Then the discovery is an-

22

nounced to the congregation in the hope that the Holy Spirit will re-work the preacher's efforts, that God will speak to God's people and make their lives more interesting than if God had left them alone.

Moving from the Biblical Text to a Sermon[3]

Do whatever praying, reading, studying, and conversing you require to stay in love with the God who has summoned you to this ministry.

Employ exegetical[4] or hermeneutical[5] strategies that enable scripture to give you something to preach that's more interesting than yourself. Try approaching a text empty-handed, willing to be surprised, daring to preach what and how scripture tells you.

Allow scripture recklessly to stoke, fund, and fuel your imagination, attentive to first impressions, allowing the text to take you places you hadn't intended to go.

If a given biblical text fails to ignite your interest or energize you, even after you have sincerely tried to allow yourself to be engaged by it, you have probably talked to the text rather than allowed the text to speak to you. Listen more open-mindedly or find another text.

If you read a biblical text and say, "Yep, makes sense. That's what I've always thought," read the text again; you've probably misunderstood. Try taking the Bible more seriously and yourself a bit less so.

Most scripture speaks primarily about God and only secondarily and derivatively about us. Take care in exhortation and application. In our culture it's too easy to psychologize and individualize, offering innocuous techniques for human improvement rather than bold claims about God's agency.

You and the Bible are in the same game. You are working with fellow preachers whose purpose is proclamation. Biblical texts will not only tell you what to say but how to say it.

Devising the Sermon for the Congregational Context

Listen to your listeners: What are they afraid of? Which conversations are they avoiding? How might the Holy Spirit be attempting to get to them? What lies do they love? With which false gods are they consorting? How are they confused about who God is and what God's up to? What is work that this congregation is being called to undertake? How are they right in ways that you're wrong? How is the gospel of Jesus Christ good news for them in their time and place? What encouragement do they need in their discipleship? What hopes, doubts, and fears do you share; which misunderstandings and delusions?

Don't assume that your listeners come to church interested in what you have to say. You'll have to slyly court, woo, cajole, even seduce them to get a theological hearing.

Hook listeners early in the sermon. In the introduction, make a promise to them that you will make good on by the end. Lure them into consideration of some problem or complication that is caused by God being in Christ, reconciling the world, rather than God being who we thought God ought to be.

Sermons are twice born: once in the preacher's study, again in the pulpit. Your sermon ought to recapitulate the journey that you made in your study. "Folks, look what God showed me this week!" Let your listeners listen in on your listening to the biblical text, inviting them into the conversation you have been having with scripture. Don't give away the end of the journey at the beginning, thus robbing your listeners of the joy of making the trip themselves.

Listeners need to be confident that you have a clear goal and can be trusted to get them there. If they remember only one thing from your sermon, what would you want that to be? Write down the intent of your sermon in one or two sentences before you compose your sermon. Respect the limits of oral communication by allowing that purpose statement ruthlessly to govern, focus, and discipline what you say.

Don't get in the way of Christ. You and your life struggles are not the main event. While your personality, voice, and bodily gestures are the media whereby Christ will speak to them, strive to be transparent so listeners can see Christ through you rather than in spite of you. As Paul put it, "For what we preach is not ourselves, but

Jesus Christ as Lord, and ourselves as your servants for Jesus' sake" (2 Cor 4:5).

Be sure your stories and illustrations illuminate the biblical text rather than wrench the sermon out of the hands of the text. Not every good story is God's. If you have a really impactful story, save it until the end.

If the text warrants, call the congregation to action, or to a decision, thereby to stride forth convinced that they have a bit part to play in God's grand salvation of the world.

Long sermons are often a sign of a preacher's arrogance in thinking that a sermon is the result of the preacher's intellect and rhetorical skill, a preacher's uncertainty that the Holy Spirit will enable the sermon to do its work, or failure to do the work required to preach a shorter sermon.

Conclude with a discovery, an "Aha!" Be sure you have made a claim about who God is for them and what God is up to with them.

Presenting the Sermon

As you preach, look and listen for nonverbal responses from your listeners. This will help you (usually unconsciously) adjust your delivery to the audience. Try speaking to the sullen teenager on the next-to-last pew whose parents forced him to be there.

Nervousness is another name for energy. Anxiety can be a sign that you respect the gravity of your vocation and the gap between us and the gospel.

Beginning a sermon with a joke is nearly always a bad idea. Including a sweet story about a child (particularly if the child is yours) risks adulterating the gospel with maudlin sentimentality.

It's annoying for you repeatedly to end statements with "Right?" or "Amen?" or "Okay?" fishing for a compliment or soliciting agreement. Anyway, you won't take seriously their response to these tedious requests for concurrence since it's been forced out of them.

Don't read your sermon; preaching is personal, bodily testimony to the gospel truth you have received, not a lecture about God.

Connect, engage, make, and keep eye contact, allow your body to communicate, thereby indicating that you really want them to hear what God has given you.

Rehearse! Practice your sermon aloud. Rehearsal makes you the first listener to your sermon and thereby enables you to make necessary adjustments. Memorize blocks of material from your sermon for more natural delivery. If you have trouble memorizing part of your sermon, it's probably a sign that the idea doesn't fit the natural flow and should therefore be moved or removed. Some of your best sermon revisions (usually deletions) occur during rehearsal.

Visualize the body movements and gestures you will make. Practice modulating your voice as you move through the sermon.

End your sermon decisively. It's the end of the journey; make the trip worthwhile. Don't repeat or summarize. Wallop them with a claim, sound a call for action, be like Jesus in so many of his parables and simply end, allowing listeners and the Holy Spirit to do the rest of the work.

After the Sermon

The worst sermon feedback is none at all.[6] Criticism of your sermon is often a sign that you have succeeded in creating a trusting, open relationship with your listeners. Some negative reactions to your sermon may be hard to hear because they are right. Listeners' anger may indicate that they are more heavily invested in the sermon's subject than you. Furthermore, whether they hear or refuse to hear (Ezek 3:11), at least they'll know that you are trying to do your job by loving both the word of God and your listeners at the same time.

Receiving little listener response? Now you know how God feels. Keep preaching. The gospel is accustomed to making its way in difficult settings.

If you listen attentively and appreciatively, then after the sermon your parishioners will tell you the sermons they're dying to hear.

Speak with care and compassion, but don't allow your need to care for your people to determine the parameters of what God may elect to say.

No sermon's over until the Holy Spirit says it's over. Sometimes the best sermons are the ones your people preach back to you weeks after you thought your sermon was done.

I'd like to know what you think of my homiletic advice to preachers. But because this is a book and not a sermon, you can't come back at me at the church door after service or over a cup of coffee tomorrow. So may I just imagine you're saying, "Yes!"

The Work of Listening

Listening to a sermon is a labor akin to the work of reading. These days, much of what we know has been spoon-fed to us from a screen, circumscribed by the comfortable information bubble in which we reside. We don't have to chew over it, be offended by it, pray, mature, meditate, or be born again for it to make sense— information rather than enlightenment.

Readers exercise empathy to get the most out of a piece of fiction. We identify with characters and (usually unconsciously) suspend our disbelief and assume a role within the story. Thereby the story doesn't merely express what we've always thought but fuels thoughts we would not have had without submitting to the story. We are lured into a different world than the one that holds our imaginations captive.

To say a sermon is "good" is somewhat akin to saying a painting is "good." The artist's work puts us to labor, attracts our attention, tempts us to see the world from an unaccustomed angle, or opens our eyes to some truth that we've previously missed. A work of art is a product of the artist's imagination but also requires the activation of our imagination. We must willingly suspend judgment about the painting's worthiness until we've done the artist the favor of trying to get a sense of what the artist is up to. I look at a painting (such as the work by Bruegel that began this book) hoping that the art will become subcutaneous, that it will get under my skin.

Not a bad way to listen to a sermon.

Talking Back to a Sermon

Talk back to your preacher to help your preacher talk to you. I've spent time on the goals of a good sermon because sometimes listeners put inappropriate questions to a sermon, showing a failure to appreciate the unique sort of public speaking that's attempted in preaching.

Over the years, I've received a fair amount of listener grousing about misfired sermons. Here's what I wish I'd had the pluck to say:

"I didn't get anything out of it."

So how much did you put into it?

"I've never heard anything like this before."

Where would you have heard truth like this? On Facebook? At a political convention? From your buddies at the bar? Give me a break. You had to get dressed and come down here at an inconvenient hour to hear truth like this. Powerful forces are at work that make sure you don't hear this news.

"That was over my head."

After all, the sermon is supposed to be about God.

"You preachers ought to spend more time in the real world, then you'd see things more realistically."

Who gets to define "realistic"?

"I'm sick and tired of hearing politics preached from the pulpit."

You mean you're tired of hearing politics that isn't yours.

"More a lecture than a sermon."

Fair criticism. Sometimes I cower before the purposes of preaching and opt for safer endeavors—like delivering a lecture. Forgive me.

"Couldn't follow."

Again, mea culpa. *The presentation of a coherent, clear, unified sermon that goes somewhere is no mean achievement.*

"Doesn't speak to the great issues of our day."

Be careful letting the world define the "great issues of the day."

"No connection with my concerns."

Are your present concerns specifically connected to the difficulty of discipleship or are they ordinary problems that come with being human? Who needs training to be just another self-concerned American with no life project greater than themselves? I'm equipping the saints for the work of ministry. Ephesians 4:12-16. You can look it up.

"Don't like the sound of your voice."

When you get to know me better you'll find that's only one of my bothersome traits that you'll have to find a way around if you expect God to speak to you through a frail, flawed, often frustrating, fellow human being.

"I'm turned off by your Southern accent."

Ditto.

"I don't like you."

What's "like" got to do with it? Church is training in how to receive God from the hands of people who're not your type.

"You didn't give us any task to do in our daily lives next week."

That's why you get paid the big bucks. It's my job to speak God's word; your job to live it. How would I know what God wants out of you next week? Preaching is the closest I've come to real work. Besides, I've got my hands full just giving you the news of what God has done so there's usually not enough time left to tell you what I think you ought to do, but I'll give it a shot if you insist.

"I'm tired of hearing about [race, politics, world hunger, gun violence, multiculturalism, money, Critical Race Theory—fill in the blanks with whatever you don't want to be bothered with]."

You and just about everybody in the Bible.

"I'm only an ordinary person. I can't do that."

Jesus thinks you are a saint. Who are we to tell Jesus what he can't make out of you?

"I don't object to what you said, but to how you said it."

I bet you object to what I said.

"That sermon was a disgrace!"

Take it up with the Lord. My being a preacher was God's idea of a good time, not mine. You think I'm preaching because I had something to get off my chest? I could have found a safer, more lucrative way to make a living, had Jesus left me to my own devices.

No negative bounce back deters God from trying to speak to you through preaching. Sermons can come at you as the old three-points-and-a-poem; a full-throated series of whoops and hollers; humble personal testimony; verse-by-verse exposition of a biblical text; feisty argument; alluring meditation; a film clip on a screen; or a reasoned, belabored explanation. Down through the ages, with dizzying diversity, preachers have offered Christ to the world, made the eternal gospel contemporary, and have found a way to bring the truth about God to speech, so that some—not as many as Jesus might like, but enough to keep the world nervous—could respond, "I hear what you are saying. Count me in."

One more thing: most listeners find it difficult decisively, conclusively, to pronounce, "That was a good sermon," because God refuses to leave a sermon's ultimate significance up to us.

Chapter 3
PREACHERS LISTENING

*Does anyone bring in a lamp in order to put it under a basket or a
bed? Shouldn't it be placed on a lampstand? Everything hidden will be
revealed, and everything secret will come out into the open.*
(Mark 4:21-22)

Preachers say no more than what we've heard. While it can
be a tough task for you to listen to a sermon, your preacher must
listen not only to you the listener but also to the biblical text,
God's word.

Tom Long, a professor and author of *Preaching from Memory
to Hope*, says that the biblical preacher's listening to the text is akin
to the preacher's entering a dark, unknown cave with a flashlight
in hand, carefully stepping into the darkness. Light falls upon
the walls of the cave, sometimes revealing blank surfaces, at other
times an unexpected image scratched into the wall, great cavern-
ous ceilings, dark, weird grottoes, stalactites, or even shimmering
gems. Then the preacher carefully retraces the path, emerges from
the mouth of the cave, waving the flashlight and joyfully calling
out, "Wait till you hear what I have discovered!"[1]

Listening to the Bible

The biblical text that challenges, judges, and encourages the church jumps upon preachers before it has its way with the congregation. While both preacher and congregation are Bible listeners, there are differences in how clergy and laity attend to a biblical text.[2] Clergy tend to read to discover authorial intent ("Mark's gospel wants us to notice that . . ."). Laity listen for personal application ("What it means for me is . . ."). Clergy linger over the historical context, cultural background, or literary patterns of a biblical text. Laity go right to contemporary, particular, and personal connections. Clergy hear a biblical text as ideas that instruct, general truth to be acknowledged and received. Laity expect the Bible to do something to them here and now.

The listening peculiar to preachers is demanded by God's intent to be in continuing conversation with God's people. Therefore, a preacher, in service to the congregation, moves from listening to an ancient biblical text to possibilities for contemporary listeners to hear the text. Respectful questions are put to scripture:

- How can I announce the claims of this biblical text in a way that will maximize people's ability to hear those divine demands?

- Who, among my people, needs to hear what this text is saying?

- Lord, how can your truth best be preached within this particular congregational context?

- What might this text intend to do among members of this congregation?

All the scriptures, Jesus says, "bear witness about me" (John 5:39). Christians actually believe that biblical interpretation and application are done, not solely through the preacher's skill or by the listeners' intelligent perception and application, but by Jesus Christ in the power of the Holy Spirit, sometimes through and sometimes in spite of the sermon. When it comes down to it, there's only one preacher: Christ who chooses to speak through preachers.

That's why just before the scriptures are read or before I stand to preach, we pray the Prayer for Illumination: "Open our hearts and minds by the power of your Holy Spirit so that as scripture is read and your word is preached we may hear what you have to say to us today. Amen."

"Come on Lord! Show up and tell us something we would never tell ourselves." Sure, I want my sermons to be meaningful for you, I just don't get to make that happen.

The Holy Spirit enables preachers to say more than we intend and to do greater work among our listeners than we know. Our hope is that what Jesus did on the road to Emmaus, he will now do to us: "Then he interpreted for them the things written about himself in all the scriptures, starting with Moses and going through all the Prophets," so that the listeners eventually exclaimed, "Weren't our hearts on fire when he spoke to us along the road and when he explained the scriptures for us?" (Luke 24:27, 32).

Although the Bible is written for you, it's not written to you. If God spoke to all of us like God spoke to Moses through a burning bush—directly, obviously—we wouldn't need to become skilled, humble biblical interpreters. Modern people have many mechanisms whereby we try to detach ourselves from scripture, which are variations on our vain attempts to keep God off our backs.[3] We tell ourselves that our problem with scripture is one of history—we are so very different from these ancient Jews, so progressed and forward thinking, living as we do at the summit of human development—Durham, NC—it's hard to hear anything of relevance from a book so old, violent, and poorly edited. (Dead gods are easier to live with than the true, living God.)

It is little wonder that many sermons quickly pivot from the biblical text and its concerns to grab hold of some area of supposedly more immediate congregational relevance. How much more personally rewarding (and intellectually easier) for a preacher to be helpful to the congregation (in the ways we think we need help) than for the preacher to submit to what the biblical text wants to talk about.

Jettisoning the biblical text as the pretext for a sermon usually tempts the preacher to dole out advice ("I'm an expert on human relationships so, rather than talk about God, let's do group therapy"), to provide commentary on contemporary social issues ("Our worries of the moment are more important than the Bible's concerns. Somebody's got to speak out on current events since the Lord won't"), or breathlessly offer a tool to make your life less miserable ("Wouldn't you rather be happy than saved, be a thriving, well-adjusted person rather than a disciple? Here's how.").

Distortion of the biblical text occurs when we preachers attempt to "apply" the biblical text to the contemporary context. Listening for scripture's unique testimony is overtaken by, "Look! Here's a biblical truth that helps you get what you think you just must have without being bothered by what Jesus wants."

"Here's what Jesus was *trying* to say in the parable of the Prodigal Son . . ." If only Jesus had been fortunate enough to attend the preacher's seminary, his preaching would have been more effective. And safer.

"Here's what Isaiah 6 *really* means." All previous interpretation of this passage, down through the church's ages, is bunk. Besides, you laity could never master the art of biblical interpretation as well as I. Thank me for making this archaic Jewish stuff relevant to people who drive Volvos.

"Though there aren't many happy marriages in scripture, marriage and family have become our substitute for discipleship, so here are three alliterative, easy-to-remember principles for how to have a happy marriage: You gotta Communicate, Care, and Cooperate."

"Jesus can deliver the anxiety-free life that you crave. Center yourself. Be at peace. Breathe deeply." If only the Twelve had you as their mindful preacher, their lives would have been less stressful.

Is there no limit to modern western intellectual arrogance? Not much. Some biblical interpretive techniques that preachers pick up in seminary are mere artful attempts to keep the biblical text at arm's length. Scripture becomes a cadaver to be dissected, then used (thereby abused) by modern people who think they know so much more than those Jews. The biblical text is so old, confusing, Jewish, and irrelevant that it's mute without the preacher's heroic efforts to say what the Bible, in its primitive bumbling, is unable to say.

Saying What the Bible Tells Us

Augustine celebrated the diversity of intent in sermons: "to teach, to delight [I love that one], and to persuade," so that listeners might hear the gospel "intelligibly, willingly and obediently."[4] Beware those who say, "All good sermons should persuade the listener to . . . ," or "Every sermon ought to lead the listener to a decision . . . ," or, "There must be a call to prophetic action." Be wary, also, of those who say, "Some pressing contemporary issue ought to be addressed." Preaching's purposes and practices are as multifarious as the Bible requires. Even in my most expansive, creative preaching, the range of my sermons will never be as rich, or will use as wide of an array of artistic and literary devices, or do as many different things to God's people, as scripture.

"My preacher's sermons all sound alike," said a listener. I suspect that while her preacher has treated a variety of biblical ideas, the preacher has not allowed the way the text speaks to guide how the preacher speaks. The preacher is always gracious, civil, and unctuous, even when the text is not.

Sermon series, in which the preacher comes up with a theme and then forages in scripture to find supporting texts, tempt the preacher to talk about what the preacher thinks the congregation may be obsessing over at the moment, revealing what the preacher is most comfy discussing and what the congregation feels most cozy hearing. Though, to be fair, we lectionary preachers can also become too comfortable by dutifully going to the lectionary each week and giving a talk on a text without active grappling with its words to our contemporary context.

Many "How to . . ." sermons swap worldly wisdom for gospel foolishness, peddling common sense as stunning revelation. Who needs to get out of bed on a Sunday for that? Rather than playing a life coach, nanny, spiritual sage, or human relations guru it is better for the preacher to dare to listen carefully and imaginatively to scripture and then humbly, dutifully tell us what has been heard.

Scripture wants not only to tap into hearers' experiences but also to give them experience they would not have had without listening to the sermon. By the instigation of scripture, sermons not only express what this congregation holds dear but also move toward where no one would go without being egged on by the biblical text.

All listening is an act of submission. In our cultural context, to submit to these ancient Jews; to bend our lives to this strange, disorderly collection of texts; to acquiesce to instruction by the church and its officials; to resist the arrogance of finding our own way; to allow others, saints both living and dead, to lead us down a path we would not, could not go on our own, requires a lifetime of training for both the preacher and listeners.

Discipline yourself not to question too quickly: "What's in this for me? How can I use this? Is this relevant?" Allow the text time to work on you before you work on it. Rather than ask yourself whether you agree, first ask: "How would my life have to change if this text and sermon were true?" Besides, the sermon's main intention is not to make Christ relevant to your life, it's to help make your life more relevant to Christ.

In our seminary chapel, I once heard a young woman preach on Jesus and the rich man (Matt 19:16-30). She told about how she left her office job to teach in the state's poorest school district. She said, "I got rid of my stuff, downsized to a two-room apartment, and am having the best life ever."

I was inspired by the testimony of this idealistic young person.

Then she ended: "We've heard how Jesus invited this man to divest and become a disciple. But he couldn't. He walked away depressed. He couldn't imagine life without his stuff. Well, I'm here to tell you. You can do this! Come on, obey Jesus. You can do this! Join me in selling all you've got. Give it to the poor and follow Jesus!"

Listening to her biblical sermon made me feel downright unsafe.

Surprising Listeners

All Christian listening exposes us to the possibility of conversion, change, detoxification, repentance (*metanoia*)—though not all preachers are upfront about it. Nobody is naturally Christian. More than asking, "Do you agree?" the gospel asks the political question: "Will you now leave where you have been living, join up, join in, and be drafted into the Jesus movement?"

Because a good sermon shares how the preacher was surprised while listening to a biblical text, expect to be startled by a biblical sermon; be disappointed when you are not. Astonishment goes hand-in-hand with revelation. If, listening to a sermon, you say, "Yes, makes perfect sense. That's what Mama taught and what I've always thought," it may be a sign that either the preacher or you haven't listened well to the biblical text.

Ask questions: What is this text doing to me? What does it expect from me? How is a dying and rising God needed to make this sermon and its claims work? What is there for God to do in the sermon? Where is the good news? How is my life, and the life of my church, being judged or encouraged by this text? Who in the congregation may be infuriated by this text? Who will be elated to hear this?

The most interesting texts for preaching are those that cause the preacher (and you, the listener) trouble. Difficult, obscure, and hard-to-understand biblical texts ignite creative listening. Much of scripture follows its own exhortation to *paroxysmon* (Greek for provoking, stiring up, egging on) one another (Heb 10:24). Sign on with Jesus; be prepared to relocate.

A preacher's accountability to scripture is somewhat akin to the performance of a musical score. The performing musician may interpret, embellish, augment, or modify the notes from what is printed but the musician is always answerable to the text. Listeners are essential to the concert, but neither they nor the preacher are the final arbiters of the fidelity of the performance; the text must have its say.

If you tell me, "That sermon was boring," I'll be a bit chagrined. If you say, "Geez, you mangled that passage," I'm in the dumps through Tuesday.

Listening in Congregational Context

We clergy do not swoop down upon the hapless congregation as visitors from Planet Preacher. In order to speak to our people, we preachers must listen to them. That's easy when you are their pastor. Embedded with them, called and paid by them, present in moments that they keep hidden from public view, you have a front-row seat from which to see their triumphs and tragedies. You know your people down deep, if you dare.

Why are so many great novelists doctors—Chekov, Bulgakov, Crichton, Maugham, and Percy? "People tell their doctor everything, even before being asked," explained a physician friend. "We see our patients naked." So do preachers, in a manner of speaking.

Trouble is, sometimes we pastors allow attentiveness to the congregation to overpower our listening to the biblical text. Traffic between text and congregational context moves in one direction. Concern for listener comprehension, relevance, and application overwhelms a preacher's (and listeners') vocation to listen to the witness of scripture. Somehow preachers must love their congregations while loving the text even more.[5]

In his *Lectures on Preaching*, Phillips Brooks said much mischief is done by the preacher who speaks of "my congregation" in a proprietary way, as if the congregation is the preacher's sole consideration.[6] Role confusion leads us to be a congregation's indulgent mama or daddy because that's easier than being their preacher. The pastor's need to love and be loved by the people eclipses the role of teller of biblical truth. Preserving affectionate, personal, individual relationships at all costs becomes the main mission of ministry.

"Preachers must be careful what they say from the pulpit," said a listener. "They can't offend those who pay his salary."

While there's some truth in the layperson's conjecture, many preachers are overly cautious and circumspect, not out of fear, but out of love. In daily pastoral contact, the pastor sees people as they are, in their often pitiful, sad, and harried lives. Who wants to make their lives more difficult?[7] Lackluster sermons result.

We preachers enjoy thinking of ourselves as caring, empathetic pastors who don't want to hurt anybody. Truth to tell, our need to people-please or be non-confrontive, all-approving affirmers of needy individuals eclipses our calling to be God's spokespersons.

At the behest of the lectionary, I preached on forgiveness. After service, a threatening voice demanded: "Do you mean to tell

42

me that Jesus expects me to *forgive* my abusive husband—who made my life hell for twenty years till I had the guts to leave?"

"Er, uh, we only have twenty minutes for these sermons and, er, spousal abuse is a terrible sin, and I d-d-don't know that I would say that, but Jesus did say seventy times seven, which has got to be a lot of forgiveness and, er, uh, he said forgive enemies and I bet you don't have a bigger enemy than your ex-husband, and . . ."

"Thanks," she said, drawing herself to her full height, "Just checking."

As she left church to rejoin the fray, I tell you it was as if the heavens opened and a dove descended saying, "Who told you that your job was to protect her from me? When you look at her, you see a victim. 'Poor victim.' Contort your voice into a whine. All moral responsibility is off your shoulders. When I look at her, I see a disciple. I'm going to turn the world upside down with the likes of her if you'll just get out of my way."

Listeners must be known, loved, and respected, but not over-much. That's why, as Phillips Brooks says, it's healthy to preach from time to time in congregations where the preacher knows nobody.[8] The preacher is thereby rescued from being muted by empathy. Time and again, the weekly climb out of the muck and mire of parochial concerns into the demanding, invigorating fresh air of the biblical text saved me from being completely engulfed by the merely contemporary and the suffocatingly personal. I was recalled for work even more challenging than love for my people; lucky me, I got to tell them the truth about God.

Every preacher who says, "My people are dear, simple folk who just can't take the tough sayings of Jesus" ought to be told, "Get over your perverted pastoral proclivity to protect them from

God. Trust Jesus to know what he is doing when he says to the likes of them, 'Listen up!'"

Better than a kowtowing, ingratiating friend who always makes you feel better, your preacher is the friend who cares enough to tell you the truth and knows you well enough to tell it in such a way that you might hear. Sorry listeners, as much as we preachers would like to be heard and received well, you're not the sole test of the "Good Sermon."

Your preacher serves you by being a servant of the Word, not by being servile to congregational expectations. Because I'm a mathematical idiot, I must hire an accountant to do my taxes. Though paid by me, my accountant doesn't only work for me. My accountant is accountable to the field of accounting, to the law, and to the IRS. My accountant serves me by keeping me out of jail for tax evasion, every now and then telling me that what I want to do, he won't do because of his commitment to do the right thing by the standards of his profession and the laws of the state.

Thus, the sole response to a sermon can't be "That really makes sense to me," but sometimes must be "Can't say that was easy to hear, but I do believe that you are trying faithfully to represent God's word to us."

Every preacher speaks under the prophetic imperative to speak up and speak out for God, whether the people who pay the preacher's salary want to hear from God at that moment or not. God's preachers are entrusted with a message that is not self-derived. The prophetic directive "You must speak my words to them, whether they listen or fail to listen, for they are rebellious" (Ezek 2:7) ought to be tattooed on every preacher's biceps.

Compared to dozens of public-speaking books, the Bible has a consistently low regard for listeners. Public-speaking books tend to be how-to cookbooks: speakers, follow these savvy principles and your listeners will lap it up. Scripture, with its many instances of bad hearing and its relentless prophetic critique of listeners, suggests that if my sermons never elicit incomprehension or negative response, that's a sure sign that I've given up too soon, that I've exchanged prattle about assorted idols for talk about the one true God of Israel and the church. If no listener has considered nailing me to some cross, then according to the preachers Matthew, Mark, Luke, and John, I've got some explaining to do.

Hard to Hear Jesus

No preacher is intentionally obscure. Every sermon intends to communicate, not obfuscate. However, it would be surprising if all your preacher's sermons are immediately comprehensible. An easily understood sermon may be an indication that its subject is not the grand, sovereign God of Israel and the church, but a sweet godlet of our own confection. Jesus's disciples frequently hadn't the foggiest idea what Jesus was talking about. Their failure to comprehend and Jesus's failure to communicate were due not simply to the disciples' intellectual limits (though I'd be the last to claim they were the brightest candles in the box) but to Jesus talking about his truth rather than what passes for truth in the world.

The best response the congregation could muster to Jesus's inaugural sermon in Capernaum? "What's this?" (Mark 1:21-28).

Sermons routinely attempt (in poet T. S. Eliot's words) a "raid on the inarticulate."[9] If they are faithful to their subject, preachers must say things that are hard to say and to understand. For example, theologian Karl Barth and I both believe this verse to be a summation of the gospel: "God was reconciling the world to himself through Christ, by not counting people's sins against them. He has trusted us with this message of reconciliation" (1 Cor 5:19). If you take that as text for a sermon, you had better warn the congregation beforehand that they are about to be lured into the deep end of the pool. Assert that God is in a homeless, vagabond rabbi who preached briefly, died violently, and rose unexpectedly (Paul's "message of reconciliation"), then you have put language under great pressure.

Paul quickly found that, in order to talk about what God was doing in the cosmos through Christ, he had to get technical; he had to use big words like *redemption, sanctification,* and *justification,* and not because everyone knew what he was talking about. Rather, he had to define and often redefine these words precisely because nobody knew their meaning until they knew Christ.

Some preachers sound more obscure as they age because they have become less anxious about being understood by everybody in every sermon. Before their last roundup, they are plumbing the mysteries of Christ more deeply or have gained, over the years, a greater appreciation for the subtleties and contradictions within the faith and are less careful to conceal them from the congregation.

Other preachers become more direct and plain-spoken over the years. One of my preaching professors once said, "The more you preach, the less you will preach," by which he meant the more experienced the preacher, the greater the preacher's respect for the limits of oral communication and therefore the less a preacher will attempt to accomplish in a sermon.

In my dotage, my sermons have grown shorter, and I tackle fewer ideas. God doesn't need my sermon to say everything God wants said. God willing, there'll be next Sunday for them, if not for me. Knowing that my best sermons are the ones that my listeners finished in ways that I couldn't, I don't have to go on and on, tie it all up neatly with a bow, repeat myself, or browbeat listeners into complete comprehension.

Occasionally, the language of sermons is hard to understand due to the preacher's insecurities and excessive need to have intellectual authority over a congregation: "Look at me! I'm smart and I read books that you (because you have real jobs) don't have time to read!"

Four allegedly biblical principles paraded on a screen imply that the preacher's skill in presenting God is better than scripture's is. If you've got a preacher who can boil down the complicated Word of God into a few catchy phrases, who needs the aid of the Holy Spirit? Christianity Lite: faith cut down to our size, belief without the bother of learning how to use the faith's peculiar language or struggling with its unique ways of seeing things.

We preachers are in the odd situation of speaking to, but also speaking beyond, our listeners—even beyond ourselves. Good preaching is aspirational, asking congregations to listen up, to expect to be stretched in their faith and understanding. We find ourselves gesturing toward that higher truth we have not yet fully grasped ourselves, enunciating that which is still beyond our own reach.

Sure, we preachers want to be heard, but sometimes the biblical text obliges us to judge, discomfort, and confuse. Infinity inhabiting a finite man, a virgin who is a mother, a baby born into the world he created, a God who dies, a dead man who lives,

47

he who had everything submitting to life as a beggar, the all-powerful one refusing to raise his hand against his killers, the best person who ever lived becoming the victim of the worst of human cruelty:[10] occasionally, incomprehension comes with the territory.

And yet, you dare.

Chapter 4

LISTENERS TO THE SERMON

God our savior . . . wants all people to be saved and to come to a knowledge of the truth. (1 Tim 2:3-4)

Everything begins with those foundational words, "And God said . . . ," followed by the creation of creatures who hear so that they may join God in conversation.

Today, when people speak of the "Word of God," they usually mean scripture. That's odd because the gospel is a living word, spoken before it was written. Reformer Martin Luther even lamented that the New Testament was written down because God's Word is a "living voice, which then soundeth forth and is heard everywhere in the world."[1] The church is a "mouth house," not a library reading room, said Luther. "Christ's kingdom is a kingdom of hearing, not a kingdom of seeing."[2] Commenting on John 20:29, Luther ridiculed those who believe that seeing is believing, saying, "Stick your eyes in your ears!"[3]

As Karl Barth famously said, it's possible to hear of God "through Russian Communism, a flute concerto, a blossoming shrub, or a dead dog."[4] Still, God has spoken definitively, most comprehensively, and personally as Jesus Christ, and Christ speaks uniquely through the conversation called preaching. Why?

"God our savior, . . . wants all people to be saved and to come to a knowledge of the truth" (1 Tim 2:3-4). Your hearing is God getting what God wants.

Preachers Devaluing Preaching

As a young pastor, I was present at a Monday morning preacher's coffee hour when the talk turned to lay reaction to sermons. "Lay people don't listen," said one older preacher. "Amen!" responded another. "Preaching is outdated, authoritarian, one-way communication that is no longer adequate to the way modern people process information," pronounced a learned novice. Right on! "Everybody is now visual rather than verbal." You said it! On and on went the clerical cataloguing of all the ways that laity have given up on sermons. Preaching is dumb.

Saintly Dr. Herbert—my preacher when I was a kid—intoned in his resonant voice, "Any of you preached last Sunday to an empty house?" Silence. "Poor laypeople. When will they ever learn of preaching's demise? How aggravating to keep showing up, still naively expecting Jesus will preach to the likes of them through the likes of us."

Why would preachers, of all people, dismiss the effectiveness of preaching, tuck preaching away on the bottom shelf of pastoral duties, and defame the listeners we're supposed to be reaching?

I'll tell you: *preaching is difficult.* A wide array of skills and talent is required. Preparation for preaching takes time; the requisite study and rehearsal are invisible to the congregation. In the pulpit, a preacher must put up or shut up: "This is testimony to what I believe, truth to which I am giving my life." No wonder preachers let themselves off the hook with, "They don't listen; they never hear."

Sometimes we preachers reassure ourselves, "Laity aren't listening," because of our reluctance to take responsibility for the power of God working through us. It's scary to be an agent of the living God; it's unnerving to have sermons do more than we intend.

"I got nothing out of that sermon" is easier for preachers to deal with than "Best sermon you ever preached. Thanks for giving me the guts to quit my job, sell the pickup, learn Spanish, and move to Honduras as a missionary."

Many times, my clerical cynicism has been overcome by listeners' hearing. The congregation that I thought was hearing-impaired performed some act so patently faithful that I, even I, was compelled to admit, "You [even you, have undeniably] heard [through me, even me] the word of truth in Christ, which is the good news of your salvation" (Eph 1:13).

Turn to the Listener

For *Sermons from Duke Chapel*, I compiled a selection of seventy-five years' worth of sermons given at Duke University Chapel.[5] Few of those historic sermons, often given by the greatest preachers of their day, indicated much concern for the context or composition of the congregation. They were pitched to anybody, anywhere, who understands English. Comparing those sermons to today's sermons demonstrates that listeners have transformed preaching more in the past several decades than in the last five hundred years.

How? Preachers woke up and exclaimed, "My goodness, there are listeners out there." Listeners now insisted that they be put front and center: "Hey preacher, connect with us as we are, where we are, or we'll take a walk."

In the 1950s, first radio and then television enabled communicators to appear more intimate with listeners. Late-night-talk-show-host familiarity, folksiness, and projected camaraderie replaced the preacher of God's word from on high. Another age's eloquent-to-the-point-of-pompous Pulpit Prince donned jeans and a T-shirt and became the cozy, conversational, aw-shucks, empathetic friend leaning over a latte to offer affable common sense.

The congregation who once anticipated pronouncements and authoritative declarations from the pulpit now demanded immediacy, spontaneity, authenticity, warmth, and genuineness.

As a mainline Protestant preacher, the demographics of most of my listeners are white and over sixty. How does the composition of my congregation account for the style, subject matter, and delivery of my sermons? Are so many of my sermons about how to find peace and relieve anxiety because that's what listeners in the last quarter of life yearn to hear? By ending so many of my sermons with a call to work for justice, do I show that I'm preaching to upper-class, educated people who enjoy thinking of themselves as resourceful, active people on top who have a responsibility to run the world? Of course I'd like to be heard, but have my sermons become overly determined by my listeners?

A veteran church observer was asked, "How long should sermons be?"

"Depends upon the listeners," Lyle replied. "Sermons are getting shorter and longer. The major factor is the median age of the congregation."

Right. The kids' short attention span can't handle more than a sound bite.

"The younger your congregation, the longer your sermon," he continued.

What?

Lyle said, "You've got a new generation of young Christians who know that they don't know. They will therefore sit for instruction in the faith. Most of you have been preaching shorter sermons because you think that your aging congregations already know. You try to evoke what they know rather than indoctrinate them into what they don't. If you've excluded fledgling, inquiring Christians from your congregation, keep preaching short sermons."[6]

Listeners rule!

Lord, have I unintentionally limited the scope of my congregation to listeners with whom I'm most comfortable, so that I don't have to grow in my preaching abilities?

Listening to the Listener

At the birth of rhetoric (the art of persuasive public speaking), Aristotle (384–322 BCE) said a good speaker adeptly analyzes the audience and crafts the speech to fit the listeners. A speech connects in three ways: (1) through the relationship between the listener and speaker (*ethos*); (2) by the content and substance of the message (*logos*); and (3) via a range of emotions and associations that are invoked in the hearers by the speaker and the message (*pathos*).[7] Aristotle then classified the various types of listeners and specified how best to appeal to what listeners are most able to hear.

Gregory the Great wrote his *Pastoral Rule* (c. 591) to equip preachers to offer "one doctrine" through "many exhortations" based on a variety of listeners.[8] Gregory lists thirty-six pairs of opposite character traits such as, "Men and women. The gluttonous and the abstinent. Those who have had experience of carnal intercourse, and those who are ignorant of it." Then Gregory gives preachers short sermons that speak to each cohort.

In the middle of the last century, two great theologians, Karl Barth and Emil Brunner, had an argument: "Just how much should a preacher appeal to and provide help for the listener?" Barth said, "Preachers, trouble not yourselves over listener peculiarities and preferences. Proclaim the one Lord, one faith, one baptism, confident that the gospel will make its way to its hearers." Brunner countered that the gospel has a God-given point of contact in the life and circumstance of each human being. Made in God's image, God meets us where we are. Careful crafting of sermons helps connect what the preacher says with what the listener needs to hear. The victor in this debate was Brunner, judged by most American preachers' anxiety about their sermons' impact upon listeners.

Rather than attempting to find some point of contact within the listener, Barth agreed with Luther's contention that God's word is always an "external word," a voice from the outside, strange and wonderful, that comes to us rather than arises out of us. Yet there's something to be said for Brunner's belief that, in the sermon, the external—not-self-derived—Word of God is spoken to engage real people, here, now. Would God speak if God did not mean to be heard, or if God had not given listeners the capacity to hear?

Though Barth was suspicious of techniques designed to drill sermons into the heads and hearts of listeners, he still believed that preachers should "make every effort to ensure that our sermon is not simply a monologue, magnificent perhaps, but not necessarily helpful to the congregation." Those to whom we speak "must constantly be present in the mind of the preacher" during sermon preparation. What the preacher knows about the congregation "will suggest unexpected ideas and associations," which will aid the preacher's study of biblical text "and will provide the element of actuality, the application of this text to the contemporary situation."[9]

While preachers have always worried about their sermons' impact, today's preachers display unprecedented concern for listeners.[10] The homiletician Fred Craddock noted that some listeners are so familiar with the Christian message that they have become anesthetized to it.[11] Craddock advised preachers to concoct sermons after an assessment of "(1) the preacher's capacity to anticipate that listener response, and (2) the preacher's capacity to shape the sermon to meet the challenge of that response."[12] In his influential, *Overhearing the Gospel*, Craddock wrote, "The listener is the place to begin." Honor the "perspective of the listener" rather than "the content to be communicated. . . . Listeners are not intruders" and the "proper business of the sermon is communication."[13] Attentiveness to hearers gives a sermon its "irreplaceable source of power": "appropriateness."[14]

Thus, preachers were told to respect the individuality of listeners and the pluralism within a congregation, and to avoid the arrogant, insensitive imposition of the pastor's point of view upon the listeners. Neither pontification to a hapless, helpless congregation, nor handing down authoritarian pronouncements, a sermon should be respectful dialogue that connects with listener experience and invites listener engagement.

The homiletician Leonora Tubbs Tisdale, in *Preaching as Local Theology and Folk Art*, urged preachers to respect and inspect the congregational setting, exegeting the congregational context as carefully as they study the biblical text.[15] Other professors attempted to characterize the consciousness of the listener, claiming to have uncovered what was going on in the listener's mind as the listener massaged the message.[16] It was Aristotle and Gregory all over again, as differences in listeners were highlighted and preachers were told that if they ignored the age, gender, class, and racial differences between themselves and their listeners, their sermons would fall on deaf ears.

In *One Gospel, Many Ears*, Joseph R. Jeter Jr. and Ronald J. Allen identified six kinds of diversity present in many congregations (age, patterns of mental operation, gender and sexual orientation, culture, relationships to the congregation, and theological viewpoints) that account for different ways of listening.[17]

Henry Mitchell praised preaching in the Black church for keeping close to the culture of the hearers and not taking an antagonistic stance against the listener in the name of "prophetic preaching." Whereas white preachers often preach condescendingly, as if the majority of their hearers were the "academically oriented" subculture counter to the "culture of the masses of folk," Black preachers keep close to the culture of the Black listener.[18]

What Do Listeners Want?

After Hans Van Der Geest interviewed more than two hundred Swiss Christians, he concluded that the most important factor in the hearing of a sermon is trust between preacher and congregation.[19] People long to hear "the dimension of deliverance," assurance that God cares and is able to deliver them from life's difficulties. Listeners also appreciate help in making meaning with a "transcendent dimension." People listen to a preacher whom they believe has been called by God, who is a dedicated pastor, and who speaks with integrity and authenticity.

When the magazine *Christianity Today* surveyed two hundred evangelical pastors and over two thousand laypeople about preaching, it found that, on the whole, laypersons were satisfied with the preaching they hear, even though many admitted that they don't always understand their pastor's sermons.[20] (Notwithstanding the recent infatuation with multimedia technology, while many pastors said that their preaching could be improved if they learned how to use visual technology, only 20 percent of the laity thought so.)

Lori Carrell sent a ten-question survey to one thousand randomly selected pastors, asking them to distribute the survey among their congregations. Of that group, 102 pastors and 497 laypersons responded. (Does the small number of pastoral participants indicate a reluctance of pastors to hear from their listeners?)[21] Carrell determined that there's quite a gap between what preachers presume they are doing in a sermon and what listeners think a sermon ought to be. Preachers are mostly clueless about listeners' expectations. Preachers believe a good sermon ought to change listeners' lives, translate the meaning of the biblical text from the past to the contemporary context, inspire, and transmit information about the Christian faith; listeners expect inspiration, life application, information, and insight.[22] When congregations were asked, "If you could get one message across to all preachers in the United States, what would it be?" their chief response was "Know your listeners."[23]

As a young pastor, I was so curious about my listeners that I administered a thirty-question survey to randomly selected members of my congregation. The survey asked them to rate various aspects of my preaching from "meaningful" to "less meaningful."[24] I intentionally adjusted some of my preaching practices (attempting to improve my eye contact, removing abstract theological terms, improving my transitions between thoughts) and then gave them the questionnaire again.

I learned that there's a great gap between what I think I'm saying in a sermon and what listeners hear. I valued careful biblical interpretation; they wanted direct application of the sermon to their daily lives. I aimed for good ideas in a sermon; they appreciated emotional impact. I presented and related a biblical text; they expected the sermon to be my personal testimony.

My parishioners were initially positive about my preaching and reluctant to criticize my sermons. (There's a "halo effect" that makes people reluctant to criticize their preacher. "Why would an astute person like me put up with a lousy preacher?") Listeners' positive assessment of my preaching dropped from the first administration of the survey to the second. I don't think that my sermons got worse; I had, through the questionnaire, produced more perceptive, critical listeners.

For example, one participant said, "I never asked myself, 'Has the preacher really been fair to this particular passage of scripture?' The more carefully I listened to your sermons, the more I found myself thinking, 'Will's stopped listening to the Bible and has gone to telling the Bible what to say.'"

Well, I asked for it.

In my next congregation, I assembled a group, read the given lection for an upcoming sermon, led a discussion, noted their reactions and insights, and asked them how they might develop a sermon on this text. At first, respondents were cautious, respectful, and uncomfortable saying too much. Once they figured out that I really cared about their responses, they became more analytical, discerning listeners.

While I occasionally garnered interesting insights from these pre-sermon groups, and I was often edified by their variety of perspectives, I was also impressed by the different responsibilities between preacher and listeners. It's doubtful that a truly courageous, challenging sermon will arise from a committee. Biblical interpretation is a complex, demanding process that not every Christian ought to be expected to master. Ordained to oversee and speak to the congregation as a whole, the pastor must submit to the disciplines of scriptural interpretation and representation of church tradition. There are limits to how much our listeners can help.[25]

In one of my early congregations, I handed out sheets of paper and pencils to every fourth person emerging from the service. Each slip of paper had the heading "What did you hear in the Sermon?" Results were discouraging. Listeners were rarely able to recall more than two ideas; sometimes the concepts they listed were nowhere to be found in my sermon manuscript. I learned from this that I was wrong to presume that sermons are about good ideas. Imagination matters more than logic. Bonhoeffer was right: the sermon enables the risen Christ to walk among his people.[26] Good sermons do more than convey information; they provoke an experience of Christ in action.

Limits of the Turn to the Listener

Sermons are polyvalent—they mean different things to different people, though all that a listener may find meaningful in a sermon is not justified by the sermon.

For instance, one Sunday I preached on Mark 6:14-29, an account of Herod's decapitation (or, if you are a Catholic, decollation) of the preacher John the Baptist. My sermon claimed that Herod moved from liking John the Baptist's preaching to killing him because he told the truth. My theme: preaching makes the church a place of truth.

In a small group discussion that evening I heard five different ways of hearing my sermon.[27] Listeners reported that they were:

1. Inspired by the reminder that the church ought to be a place where the truth is told, whether we like hearing it or not.

2. Put off by the preacher's comparison of his preaching to that of John the Baptist's.

3. Annoyed by the preacher's implied criticism of the prevarication of contemporary American political leaders.

4. In agreement with the preacher's call for today's pastors to be more like the truth-telling prophets of old.

5. Thankful that, unlike Jews back then, we live in a democracy where our rulers respect and protect our freedom of religion.

The first four responses are justified by the content, apparent intent, and tone of the biblical text, as well as by the sermon's interpretation of the text. Listener Number Five's response is not; it diverges too far from the character of the biblical narrative and the assertions of the sermon and is an overbearing imposition of the listener's biases upon text and sermon.

So, to say that listeners hear different things in the same sermon is not to say that what every listener hears is valid, fair, and justifiable. The appropriateness of the listener's judgments must be within the parameters of meaning that are offered by the text and sermon.[28]

Too great a concern for relevance to the needs and questions of the listener implies that the listener's self-defined needs set the agenda of the sermon. The gospel is reduced to another technique for self-improvement, just one more human relations resource. Listening for God is replaced by commentary on the human experience of God.

Isn't it a bit arrogant for preachers to assume that we know the minds of our listeners better than they are known by the listeners themselves? Our listeners are not problems to be solved, they are arcane, secretive, wondrous mysteries. The way God works in their lives is known only to God (Col 3:3). Truth to tell, we preachers are more likely to discover the secrets of a biblical text than the hidden paths into our listeners' hearts and minds. Because of the effusive revelation of a relentlessly self-revealing God, we know more of Christ than we know for sure about either ourselves or our listeners.

It was my duty to preach four back-to-back baccalaureate sermons at Duke before each year's commencement. To prime myself for this task, I randomly selected graduating seniors, asking them, "What are you thinking on the eve of graduation?"

After an hour of conversation about their hopes and fears, one of the graduates said, "When you speak, I hope you'll tell us what you know rather than worry too much about what we're thinking.

I don't know if I'm a Christian. I do know that on graduation weekend we're going to be exposed to lots of advice from old guys like you. Don't give us advice. The one thing you're supposed to know about is God. I hope you'll talk about God, not us."

Preachers speak about God, not because we have privileged access to listeners, but because God speaks to preachers in order that God may speak to those who ask, "Any word from the Lord?" (Jer 37:16-17).

Converting Conversation

Even if we succeed in categorizing, analyzing, and understanding our listeners, there's a good chance that our categorization will be messed up by the end of the sermon. The gospel of Jesus Christ may meet us where we are but rarely leaves us there. When God speaks, something (or someone) new is created, recreated (Gen 1). By preaching, "Repent, believe the gospel" (Mark 1:15), Jesus preached *metanoia*, the relinquishment of old notions and the embrace of the new—in short, conversion.

As a Duke undergrad said to me after a service, "I'm not the same as I was when you started talking."

A favorite self-defense against conversion is "Pastor, you just don't understand me because you've never [fill in the blanks: suffered as great a loss as mine, been addicted to alcohol, gone through a divorce, experienced injustice, gotten depressed, suffered an eating disorder, been afflicted with rebellious kids, etc.]." They thereby reassure themselves that I couldn't possibly have anything to say about their situation because I'm not a certified member of their cherished marginalized group.

All of us have multiple protective devices that we use to guard ourselves against what's uncomfortable to hear. As I've said, it's a lifelong challenge to receive Christ from the hands of another.

Had we the time, I could make a case that one of the best ways to receive a gift from a sermon is to be fortunate enough to have a preacher who is of a different racial, gender, age, psychological, or victimized group than yours. Cultivate a willingness to be surprised that, in spite of the dissimilarities between you and your preacher, God enables you to hear God through this preacher nevertheless.

Christ Will Have His Say

We listeners do well to remind ourselves that, while Jesus sought to communicate, he never gave the listener control of the conversation. A listener's openness is neither the criterion nor the validation of God's Word as God's word. While Christ urges us to "listen," we are not saved even by skillful listening. Listeners either hear or do not hear for a wide array of reasons, some having to do with the imperfections of the preacher, some owing to limits of the listeners, and some having to do with challenges inherent in the "external word," the gospel of Jesus Christ. The listener who responds to a sermon with "I just don't understand" may have understood all too well. "I didn't hear" could mean, "I've heard, but I don't like it."

Preaching is more difficult than most public speaking, not because of the audience but because of Jesus. Once, a listener was angered by a sermon I gave in Duke Chapel. As she unloaded on me, a gaggle of exiting students gathered (what young adult doesn't enjoy seeing a congregation rough up a preacher?). After she stormed off, one of the students smirked, "Looks like somebody didn't want to be as close to Jesus as she first thought."

Why couldn't I come up with that grand retort?

In taking our listeners seriously, in utilizing our pastoral opportunities to know listeners in depth, we must not be overwhelmed by their variety. We must know them, not simply by their worldly labels, but as they are known *in Christ*. They are those toward whom God has turned. For all their differences and diverse backgrounds, would Christ have called them had he not intended to speak to them?

Through baptism, listener identities—some that the world imposes, some self-selected—are being reconfigured, relativized, transformed, or washed away so that they recognize themselves as "a royal priesthood, a holy nation, a people who are God's own possession . . . so that you may speak of the wonderful acts of the one who called you out of darkness into his amazing light" (1 Pet 2:9).

Because of the diversity (and perversity!) of our listeners, homiletics professors will never be able to devise a knock-down, sure-fire method for successfully communicating the gospel. Christ is the one, true preacher, the ultimate instigator of hearing. Christ speaks to and is heard by whom he will. As Martin Luther said, the gospel is "like a moving shower of rain which strikes what it strikes and misses what it misses."[29] Still, in spite of all the reasons why listeners may not hear a sermon, we may listen with confidence that a relentlessly revealing God is determined to be heard.

You think you are sitting through a sermon because you want to, fancying yourself to be in control of the communication, blithely supposing that you can filter, unplug, hit delete anytime you like. No, if you can decide what God can say to you, that god can never save you.

Yet we do hear. What a comfort to know that our relationship with God is not in our hands, not just another laborious assignment. It's up to God to keep the God/human conversation going and every time you hear something in a sermon you know, God does.

"I had my people pegged as a conglomeration of self-interested, materialistic consumers but then Jesus came along and made them into a church with a heart for mission," said a preacher, with a smile.

God's relentless vocalizing bids us preachers not to take our listeners' current status or their adamant refusals too seriously. Whether defiant or diffident, their "No" is bracketed by God's dramatic, repeated "Yes." While admitting that many fail to listen to sermons, Luther celebrated, "Nonetheless, there will always be a few who will hear God's precious Word with delight; and for their sakes, too, we must preach it. For since God provides people whom He orders to preach, He will surely also supply and send listeners who will take this instruction to heart."[30] Daring listeners, potential hearers—God's gift to preachers and to the world.

Jesus told a parable about a rich man who died and went (of course) straight to hell and a poor man who, in death, is carried to the bosom of Abraham (Luke 16:19-31). In torment, the rich man begs Abraham to send once-poor Lazarus to warn his wealthy relations of the punishment to come. "Forget it!" scoffs Abraham. Those who didn't listen to Moses and the prophets wouldn't listen even to a preacher come back from the dead.

Chapter 4

A smile breaks out on the face of the church. Father Abraham misjudged us. Despite our differences, and all the reasons we're lousy listeners, here we are, still daring to listen to an outrageous story told to us by the only preacher who ever came back from the dead.

Chapter 5

HEARERS OF THE SERMON

We also thank God constantly for this: when you accepted God's word that you heard from us, you welcomed it for what it truly is. Instead of accepting it as a human message, you accepted it as God's message, and it continues to work in you who are believers. (1 Thess 2:13)

I listened to a sermon by Fleming Rutledge that opened with, "I'm sure you've heard said that the Old Testament is about judgement and the New Testament about grace."[1] Prompted by Jeremiah and Paul she said, "If we think along these lines, we will have made a big mistake." Fleming then took a potentially conflicted notion—the wrath of God—matched it with the movie *Traffic*, threw in a reference to a Cormac McCarthy novel, and spoke of Jesus as engaged in "mortal combat with Satan," because "God is opposed to any power that keeps out of relationship with God." I heard.

A few weeks later at the same church, I listened to a sermon by a young man who preached with some vitality and way too much earnestness. His alleged text was from one of the Minor Prophets; I forget which. Who cares; the prophet made only a cameo appearance in the sermon and was given no work to do. The preacher announced that the prophet's concern was "justice for the oppressed," which he defined as "liberation," "self-determination," and a "sense of self-worth." High-sounding, vacuous words— "spirituality," "trauma," and "lament"—filled the air. Having given away his theme in the first few minutes, the sermon staggered from one triviality to another and died.

Imperatives—"should," "ought," and "must"—were flung at us as the preacher insisted that we get off our duffs and get busy on behalf of justice since God wasn't, though we suspected that the preacher was exempt from such action because he assumed that if he simply told us to be just he had done something himself. I listened but heard nothing that I couldn't have heard as well (better) elsewhere.

I prefer to think that I failed to hear because I'm such a discerning listener. Who knows? My mishearing could be a function of my sinful inclination to tell God what I want to hear and from whom. So, when I hear "original sin," I think not of some ancient Christian doctrine of innate human sinfulness but rather of my own unoriginal bundle of biases, prejudices, and pride that close my ears to God. To paraphrase Paul, the hearing that I would do, I cannot. Who shall deliver me from my impairment (Rom 7:24)? Who? The only preacher who ever came back from the dead.

Hard of Hearing

Kate Murphy's research suggests that our ears are not as good as they once were.[2] In two decades, the average amount of time for conversational listening to each other has gone down by almost half, from 42 percent to 24 percent. A 2018 survey of twenty thousand Americans reveals that half said they had few meaningful in-person exchanges. Youth who are heavy users of social media are 27 percent more likely to suffer from clinical depression. Never have so many been so technically connected, yet so alone. A study conducted by Microsoft found that since the year 2000, the average attention span has dropped from twelve to eight seconds.

"If anyone tells a story longer than thirty seconds, heads bow not in contemplation but to read texts, check sports scores or see what's trending online," says Murphy. She blames decreasing auditory abilities not on media technology, as might I, but on a culture of "aggressive personal marketing," where "to be silent is to fall behind. To listen is to miss an opportunity to advance your brand and make your mark. . . . Listening is often regarded as talking's meek counterpart." Murphy also says that "value is placed on what you project, not what you absorb. . . . The very image of success and power today is someone miked up and prowling around a stage or orating from behind a podium. Giving a TED talk . . . is living the dream."[3]

Though God created us with two ears and one mouth, listening is increasingly a physical challenge, according to Murphy's research. Sound levels now average eighty decibels at restaurants, easily overwhelming the average conversation (sixty decibels); stores such as H&M and Zara have noise levels up to ninety decibels. The World Health Organization says that chronic headphone abuse puts 1.1 billion young people at risk of hearing loss. Here comes "generation deaf."[4]

Still, it's my hunch that failure to hear a sermon is due to factors other than physical.

Speak, Lord, Your Servant Is Listening, Sort Of

"Now the boy Samuel was serving the Lord under Eli" (1 Sam 3:1), a little boy apprenticed to old Eli the priest. Being a priest—intermediary between God and people—was no easy task in those days because "the LORD's word was rare."

Had Yahweh become fatigued by speaking and yet receiving so little listener feedback? Or perhaps God had continued to reveal God's self, but the people had lost the courage to listen. First Samuel is too good a storyteller to step aside and sermonize. All we know for sure is that there was a paucity of God's Word, a sermon shortage.

One night, as everyone slept in the priestly quarters, little Samuel heard a voice calling, to which he responded, "I'm here."

(Sermon aside: It is fascinating, in scripture, how often people hear God when they sleep—Acts 10:10; 12:6; and so on. Isn't this a comforting thought for any churchgoer who's been a somnambulant listener—and who hasn't been in some sermon or another? Be careful you sleepers-through-sermons. While you're dozing, maybe God will take advantage of your vulnerability and speak.)

Samuel runs to Eli and says, "I'm here. You called?" (1 Sam 3:5).

"I didn't call you," says Eli. "Go back and lie down."

Again, the boy hears, "Samuel!"

(Digression: As those familiar with the Bible know, repetitious calling of one's name is a sure sign of a call story, of vocation: "Moses, Moses" [Exod 3], "Saul, Saul" [Acts 9:4]. Samuel has been summoned, not by the aging priest but by God, enlisted to be given a task. For most of us, it takes at least two or three summons before God gets our attention.)

70

Again, little Samuel goes to Eli asking, "You called?" Again, Eli tells him to go back to sleep.

(Here I will resist the temptation to launch into a sermonette on how the younger generation is sometimes called to wake up their elders even though we old folks would rather Rip Van Winkle through the revolution.)

The narrator explains: "Now Samuel didn't yet know the Lord, and the LORD's word hadn't yet been revealed to him" (1 Sam 3:7).

Yet a third time, "the LORD called Samuel. He got up, went to Eli, and said, 'I'm here. You called me?'"

(I shall defy my inclination to expound that, for most of us, the Lord will keep knocking on our door, repeatedly calling our names before we're able to say, "You called?")

Eli realized the Lord was calling for the boy. So, Eli said to Samuel: "Go and lie down. If he calls you, say, 'Speak, LORD. Your servant is listening.'"

(As a child I remember our pastor preaching that "when God calls, God calls us by our very own name, not by somebody else's name, just like God called little Samuel." When God's general claims upon humanity become specifically addressed to you and you hear your name called, that's when you hear, and I mean *really* hear a sermon.)

The fourth time his name is called, Samuel replied, "Speak. Your servant is listening" (1 Sam 3:10). It's the prayer that ought to be on a Christian's lips at the beginning of every sermon.

(Fellow senior citizens note: even though young Samuel receives a direct address from God, the kid is still dependent upon the aged Eli to interpret it for him. Though we old guys are on our way out, we can still help the young in their conversations with

71

God.[5] There are so many good sermons in this short, vivid story but so little time to preach them.)

"I am about to do something in Israel that will make the ears of all who hear it tingle!" says the Lord (1 Sam 3:11). God speaks judgment against the house of Eli because of the sins of his sons, words that neither Samuel nor Eli want to hear. Young Samuel is commissioned by God to tell Eli of the coming cataclysm that's about to break upon his family, words no preacher willingly speaks.

"'What did he say to you?'" Eli asked. "'Don't hide anything from me . . .' So Samuel told him everything and hid nothing from him."

"He is the Lord," Eli said. "He will do as he pleases" (1 Sam 3:17-18).

(Closing Prayer: *God make me as courageous a preacher as little Samuel, as brave a listener as Eli.*)

Insights gleaned for would-be hearers of God:

- God's voice, divine revelation, is an intrusion, a word that comes to us rather than being initiated by us.

- God's word is often given to the least likely of recipients. (Why did God speak so vividly to the untrained, inexperienced youth rather than to the credentialed, authorized, mature priest?)

- The young sometimes hear fresh revelation from God but don't recognize it as God's word to them without interpretive assistance from those with more experience of God.

- Reception of God's revelation is rarely at first hearing.

- You don't have to be intentionally listening for God in order to hear God.

- God's word usually comes to us through others, those who dare to tell us truth we wouldn't tell ourselves.

- Sometimes God speaks to the uncredentialed and the inexperienced words that we professional, seminary-trained ordained wish God would speak to us.

Samuel's career in prophecy began with hearing. We are told that when Samuel grew up to be a prophet, "the LORD was with him, not allowing any of his words to fail" (or as the RSV more vividly puts it: "none of his words fall to the ground" [1 Sam 3:19]), a more successful preaching career than most of us enjoy.

Miraculous Hearing

The Greek word *akouo* in our English New Testament is translated as "hear," but it can also be rendered as "listen." The same range of meaning is evoked by *shema* (e.g., Deut 6:4) in Hebrew. Both "hear" and "listen" are usually to be taken imperatively as in "Listen up!" or even as "Obey" (Exod 19:5; Jer 7:23-24), as when Jesus says, "Let anyone with ears to hear listen!" (Mark 4:9).

The prophets sometimes bewail, at other times ridicule people whom God has given ears but who don't hear (Jer 5:21; Ezek 12:2; Isa 42:20; 43:8). Israel's repeated refusal to listen is bemoaned (Deut 8:20; Josh 5:6; Zech 7:11-12). No contemporary preacher's lament of listener rebuff is as tough as Israel's disarmingly, admirably honest self-critique of its difficulties when listening for God.

Sometimes a failure to listen up is attributed to God's judgment (Isa 6:10; Deut 29:4), whereby God withdraws from God's people the capacity to hear, though refusal to hear may be punishment of our own devising. Prophetic criticism of Israel's periodic heedlessness is accompanied by the prophetic promise that when

God turns back toward Israel there will be hearing (Isa 32:3), whereby the God-Israel conversation may continue into eternity.

I don't know whether it's encouraging or discouraging to contemporary listeners that scripture (by my estimate) records more instances of hearing failure and listener rejection than communication success. Get nothing out of a sermon? You're in distinguished company. Felix and Agrippa were powerful, presumably classically educated, governmental leaders. Paul preached eloquently to Felix and Drusilla, daring to lecture them on "upright behavior, self-control, and the coming judgment," and got the cold shoulder that a truthful preacher would receive from today's politicians (Acts 24). After Paul smacked King Agrippa with his most powerful sermon, the best Agrippa could say was that Paul had not quite convinced him (Acts 26:28). Paul chalked it up as a "No."

Although there's little evidence that people actually responded in specific, measurable ways to the prophetic preachers' calls to repent, that is to change heart and life, prophets kept talking, leaving us some of the pushiest, most eloquent poetry ever heard, or refused to be heard. Contemporary preachers, frustrated by lack of listener response, take heart! Whether they hear or refuse to hear (Ezek 2:5, 7), listener response doesn't place a boundary around what God says to God's people through God's preachers. Current listeners, exasperated by an inability to make sense of sermons, be of good cheer! Your auditory limitations don't stump God.

Please note that God's word comes to, rather than from, prophets: "I set you apart . . . I made you a prophet. . . . I am with you . . . ; I appointed . . . you shall speak whatever I command . . . I am with you . . . I am putting words in your mouth" (Jer 1:4-9).

Thus, Amos speaks, not because he has something to get off his chest but rather because God has something to say: "A lion roars; who will not fear? The Lord God has spoken; who can but prophesy?" (Amos 3:8). Beaten up by the rigors of the preaching life, Jeremiah resolves not to speak again for God, but there's a fire in his belly: "I'm drained trying to contain it; I'm unable to do it" (Jer 20:9). Ezekiel hears God say, "I've made you a lookout for the house of Israel. When you hear a word from me, deliver my warning" (Ezek 3:17).

Prophets are distinguished by their lack of originality; they never get to preach what they personally might like to say. When the congregation whines about something said in a sermon, preachers discover powerful freedom in the rejoinder, "Though I'm no Amos, Jeremiah, or Hosea, just like them, being a preacher wasn't my idea of a good time. I preach what I've been told. Got a problem with me as your preacher? Take it up with the Lord."

Hearing is not an exclusively human work. The New Testament frequently stresses that it's impossible to hear God without "faith," God's gift, grace (Acts 4:4; Rom 10:17; 1 Thess 2:13). We're not supposed to listen for God unassisted.

Again, there's that crazy farmer who—without carefully preparing good, receptive soil—just started slinging seed. Though most of the seed was wasted, what we might judge to be a farming failure, Jesus celebrates as miraculous harvest (Matt 13:1-9).

Admittedly, speakers on behalf of false gods tend to be more successful and useful than speakers for the Trinity, because advocates for false gods—idols—don't have to deal with facts, the stubborn, noncompliant reality of the God who is rather than the myriad of user-friendly gods we wish there were. That's why I've got lots of explanations for why people don't hear, few reasons—none of them non-miraculous—for why they do.

When we hear, we know not only that God has connected with us but also that God is other than us. Hearing is an encounter with otherness, not merely a projection of what's going on inside of us. In conversation we have been turned away from our relentless scanning of our egos, our incessant soliloquy, and our ears perk up toward a word that has come to us. We are in ecstasy, a word directly from Greek (*exstasis*), meaning to stand outside ourselves, a feat so difficult for us moderns.

Elaine Pagels grew up in a home where her disbelieving father believed that religion had been supplanted by Darwin.[6] At age fifteen, Pagels went with friends to a Billy Graham crusade in San Francisco. Graham opened his sermon by naming American sin: nuclear armaments and racism. It was the first time Pagels had heard her nation criticized, held to a higher standard than national self-interest. A seed was planted and took root; Pagels became a Christian. Sometimes, in the hands of the Holy Spirit, even to hear what Christianity is against leads listeners toward what it's for.

Though failure is expected, our job as preachers is Sunday-upon-Sunday to sling the seed; the harvest is up to God. Preachers don't work alone. It's not a sermon until the Holy Spirit shows up, rips a sermon out of my hands, makes a dull religious lecture into pyrotechnic proclamation, and enables my words to cavort through the exposed congregation. Like I said, if anybody hears, it's a miracle.

Demonstration of Incarnation

The Word of God comes from God, through the lips of thoroughly human (and, if you know us personally, very flawed) preachers, to God's (faulty, contentious, obdurate, truth-resistant) people. Preaching is the typically incarnational performance one expects from preacher Jesus, fully God and fully human, God making human words God's, God refusing to be God without us.

We found in the pandemic, with our attempts at virtual preaching and online worship, that an incarnational faith makes bodies and bodily congregating essential for preaching. A virtual sermon, viewed mostly by individuals from outside the physical Body of Christ, is a simulation, not much better than a sermon read from a book. The body of the preacher and the bodies of the congregation are integral to Christian hearing. Christmas, the Incarnation, assures that God loves us enough to communicate bodily. God wants so much to be in conversation with us that God takes on our body so that we might become Christ's Body, the way Christ takes up room in the world.

A sermon is a public, bodily, corporate, corporeal event in the here and now. If asked, "What was your sermon about last Sunday; we were out of town," I am justified in responding, "Sorry, you missed it."

Hearing Jesus

It's Jesus who makes our hearing more conflicted and our lives more difficult, not preachers. Nothing a preacher can say to you is as judgmental, infuriating, and fearful as that which Jesus routinely says in his preachments. If the New Testament be believed, Jesus is among us not only to comfort but also to call, not just to sooth but to summon, just like God commissioned young Samuel or murderous Moses.

The God who, through a burning bush that was not consumed, told Moses to go, talk back to Pharaoh, who told Eli that his family would fall apart, is the same who preached the Sermon on the Mount (Matt 5), telling us to love our enemies, bless those who persecute us, thus complicating the lives of the young and breaking the hearts of many a parent (Matt 10:35).

If Jesus could have said it more accessibly, in a way more immediately understood, he would have. No preacher ought to make Jesus more user-friendly than he intends to be.

Secrets have "been given to you, but to those who are outside . . . they can look and see but have no insight, and they can hear but not understand" (Mark 4:12). From this I infer that Jesus is best comprehended from the inside, building upon what you've heard, gradually inculcating the requisite posture, disciplines, and listening skills, rising to even greater understanding of his mysteries by degree, explaining Jesus through the inexplicable.

"Listen carefully!" (Luke 8:18). Jesus goes on to say that if we listen, we'll be given even more but if we fail to listen, even the little we've heard will be taken away. Not sure what Jesus meant by that. Maybe this isn't a warning but an encouragement; the better we learn to listen, the more we'll hear.

Jesus Will Preach

You've got a challenge as a listener. You have no prior, privileged information on what a preacher intends to say or why. Then there is your bundle of prejudices, biases, and hindrances to hearing.

On the other hand, you have some things in your favor. The preacher is risking a bold move that most folks never venture: standing up in front of a group, speaking about no less potentially conflicted subject than Jesus. So, the preacher must really want to make contact with you.

Because you're a Christian, you know that you need all the equipment for discipleship that you can get so you'll probably make an effort to hear. After all, though you have a full life with lots of alternatives, yet there you are. You've shown up. You're listening rather than talking. That's a start.

Your chief hope for success in hearing is a relentlessly revealing, resourceful God who has, time and again, shown a willingness to go to ridiculous lengths (cross and resurrection) to be in conversation with the likes of you. Christ, the pushy preacher, incessant revealer, the caller of the inept, the keeper of no secrets makes your hearing possible (Mark 4:22).

There's that wonderful story of Jesus visiting the home of his friends Mary and Martha (Luke 10:38-42). While Martha bustles about in the kitchen, graciously preparing a meal for peripatetic Jesus, Mary sits at Jesus's feet, listening. Luke says Martha was "preoccupied" whipping up a meal. Jesus praised Mary but called Martha "distracted." Is Jesus saying that listening to him is more important (and difficult) than hospitably serving him? You make the call.

Let's just say that some of us are like Mary. We enjoy sitting quietly and listening to Jesus. Others are activists who, like Martha, are impatient with listening and are itching to get busy working for Jesus. Some like nothing better than settling back and hoping for a good sermon, and others of us squirm, messing with our cell phones, eager for the preacher to be done so we can get on with living for, rather than listening to, Jesus.

Consider carefully that Jesus speaks to *both* sisters in their differences, barges in during suppertime, cares for and engages in intimate, inopportune conversation with both Mary and Martha. Still does.

When it comes down to it, there's only one preacher—Jesus. That's why scripture offers little advice for how to hear a sermon. If you hear, it's more a testimony to what Jesus does than the skill or earnestness of either preacher or listener. While I'm reluctant to offer general rules for listeners, I'll venture this: *Listen to a sermon as you listen, not as I tell you that you ought to listen.*

How do you engage in conversation? What are some aspects of your personality that Jesus might leverage to make you a good listener? What tricks and techniques do you use when you are trying to stay interested in what another person says to you? What signals do you send your conversation partner to indicate your participation in the conversation?

"Do you really think young kids ought to be brought to Sunday worship?" a mother asked. "They just don't get much out of it."

Taking up the challenge, I knelt down to her six-year-old daughter and asked, "Grace, what did you get out my sermon today?"

"Today I heard about Jesus getting mad because the disciples kept making him sad. But he kept being their friend. Was your sermon about us?"

Point, set, match. Who could ask for a better listener? A six-year-old multitasker, proof positive of the gift of the Holy Spirit, a child aptly named.

Jesus, Initiator of Conversation

We are the recipients rather than the initiators of conversation with Jesus. On the first Easter morning Mary Magdalene mistook the risen Christ for a gardener until she heard Jesus call her name (John 20:1ff.). Mary ran breathlessly back to the other disciples and preached, "I've seen the Lord" (John 20:18). She could have as well said, "Hey guys, listen up! The conversation with Jesus hasn't ended; it's just been restarted."

That evening the disciples were hunkered down like frightened bunnies behind locked doors (John 20:19-30). Never one to be hindered by our craving for self-protection, the risen Christ came and stood among them. Thomas declared, "Unless I see the nail marks in his hands, put my finger in the wounds left by the nails, and put my hand into his side, I won't believe" (20:25). Jesus offered Thomas tangible, empirical evidence: "Put your finger here. Look at my hands. Put your hand into my side. No more disbelief. Believe!" We don't know if Thomas took Jesus up on his offer to jab his finger in the hole in his side. Just hearing the loving invitation "Believe!" was enough for Thomas to exclaim, "My Lord and my God!" Hearing is believing.

So, John ends by stating the whole point of writing his Gospel: "These things are written so that you will believe that Jesus is the Christ, God's Son, and that believing, you will have life in his name" (John 20:31). Jesus promises to tell us enough to enable us to believe.

When Simon Peter saw a ghostly figure out on the roaring waves he said, "Lord, if it's you, order me to come to you on the sea." Jesus said, "Come." Simon had traveled with Jesus for months but couldn't be sure it was Jesus until he heard him (Matt 14:28-29). Jesus called, "Come," just as he had earlier called Simon to come be a disciple; Simon ventured forth based on nothing more than what he had heard (Matt 4:19).

As a pastor, I have gained much respect for the resourcefulness of Christ's determination to get a hearing, having heard so many stories of people who didn't want to hear God, weren't thinking about God, who, despite themselves, heard. Hospital men's restrooms, dormitory bedrooms at midnight, lying in the gutter after a major disappointment, pushing a shopping cart at Costco, reading a book by C. S. Lewis or even J. K. Rowling.[7] Don't think you are safe just because you're not in church sitting through a sermon. Jesus will have his say; he will be heard.

While there are many reasons why people neither listen to nor get much out of sermons, God promises:

> My word that comes from my mouth;
> it does not return to me empty.
> Instead, it does what I want,
> and accomplishes what I intend. (Isa 55:11)

"Go to Nineveh, to the people you despise and preach to them!" God commands Jonah. There are negotiations, divine threats, ingestion by a great fish, finally—after being vomited up on a beach—Jonah relents, takes a shower, goes to Nineveh and becomes the world's most reluctant evangelist. With a bad attitude, Jonah preaches the shortest, sorriest sermon in history: "Forty days and Nineveh will be overthrown!" There, I've said it. To hell with you all.

In response the king repents, the people repent, even the livestock. God took the worst excuse of a sermon and made it one of the most fruitful in history.

Jonah's reaction? He gets depressed. "I knew you might pull a stunt like this!" Jonah raged. "Merciful as you are even to those I hate." Downright galling when the folk hear and relent despite a preacher's contempt for and frustration with the listeners.

God was upfront with Ezekiel about the quality of his targeted audience:

> He said to me: Human one, I'm sending you to the Israelites, a traitorous and rebellious people. They and their ancestors have been rebelling against me to this very day. I'm sending you to their hard-headed and hard-hearted descendants, and you will say to them: The Lord God proclaims. Whether they listen or whether they refuse, since they are a household of rebels, they will know that a prophet has been among them.
>
> And as for you, human one, don't be afraid! . . . You'll speak my words to them whether they listen or whether they refuse. They are just a household of rebels! (Ezek 2:3-8)

They won't admit it, but this passage is a great favorite among preachers with its characterization of you listeners as "hardheaded and hard-hearted" "rebels" to whom we must "speak my words . . . whether they listen or whether they refuse." If they pillory you, refuse to pay your travel allowance, fire you, or worse, as you finally pull out of the church parking lot, tires kicking up gravel, you can look at your persecutors through your rear-view mirror and say that at least these hard-hearts "know that a prophet has been among them."

That's some consolation for a failed preacher, I guess.

Still, when Jesus "opened the scriptures" to his own disciples on the Easter evening walk to Emmaus, although he judged them to be afflicted with "dull minds," Jesus kept talking, broke bread with them, and they understood (Luke 24:25). Listeners ought to love this passage. If you hear a sermon, it's proof that Isaiah was right: "I was found by those who didn't look for me; I revealed myself to those who didn't ask for me" (Isa 65:1).

Because of who Jesus is and how he works, you can hear! Our God is not coy, apophatic, mysterious, or arcane. Hey, if you are still reading this book, alone or in a group, it's probably because you believe that Jesus wants to tell you something and that he is undeterred even by a preacher like me.

Harry Emerson Fosdick recalled the listener who said, after hearing John Wesley preaching to the multitude at Moorefields al fresco, "When he did speak, I thought his whole discourse was aimed at me."[8] Ah, the risen Christ at work.

Relating to the Preacher

While he was all for a well-reasoned, thoughtful speech, Aristotle said that *ethos*—a speaker's character and the listener's relationship with the speaker—aided hearing more than any other factor. Preaching is usually abetted by preacher and listener being in relationship. You need not know a novelist fully to enjoy and profit from his or her novel, and in no way does the novelist need to know you. Preaching is otherwise. Your congregation can out-local any other human organization. Sure, there are better communicators than your preacher, but none more knowledgeable about you. When one who is known speaks to those who are known, the message is more likely to be heard (and less able to be resisted) by its recipients.

The truth a preacher speaks is personified, first in Christ, then through the preacher. Though a sermon is considerably more than "just my personal opinion," hearers are right to expect that they are hearing what the preacher has personally discovered. Testimony. Witness. John 1. You are witnessing the Word embodied in a frail, fellow listener and shining forth into the world through someone who says, "This isn't just truth I've heard; it's truth that I'm trying to be true to by the way I live."

That's why most listeners don't like sermons that are read to them. Eye contact is essential, not only as visual acknowledgment of the listeners but also because preaching is supposed to be testimony, witness in ways that words, read off a page, even when they are the preacher's own, heartfelt words, seem less than personal, embodied truth.

Sappy listeners sometimes urge their preacher just to "share what's on your heart," as if the point of the sermon is to give us a peek into the preacher's mental health. No. In listening to a sermon, we're listening for more than spilling of clerical guts. A preacher witnesses, testifies to the preacher's experience of One more significant than the preacher.

Still, while "we don't preach about ourselves, but instead, we preach about Jesus Christ as Lord, . . ." (2 Cor 4:5), we preach that to which we ourselves have personally, visibly committed.

Many young adult listeners have told me that they want a preacher to be "authentic." I tremble when I hear them say that. Sincerity and authenticity are often in the eyes of the beholder. I think I'm sincerely, authentically preaching what I have heard the biblical text say, but maybe I'd be the last to know for sure.

When listeners demand "sincerity" or "authenticity" from their preachers, they are justly asking for congruence between the preacher's talk and walk. When there's a disjuncture between the faith that a preacher speaks of and the life that the preacher is struggling to live, well, there's a problem.

I preached passionately about how "materialism and greed run rampant in American society." I got 'em told, if I say so myself. After service a member of the church finance committee said, "So glad you are speaking up on important social issues. Also, I'm pleased that (inferring from your sermon) you won't be upset when there's no salary increase next year. Thanks to your prophetic preaching, our budget is broke."

Oops.

If your preacher has a winning personality, good for you. However, if you're turned off by your preacher's demeanor or temperament, have reservations about your preacher's dress, grammar, hair, or footwear, don't despair. God has a long history of speaking through the unlikable, abrasive, unattractive, and hard-to-get-along-with whom none of us would invite to speak at the banquet if we, rather than Jesus, were the host.

Read the Bible.

Chapter 6

RESPONDING TO
THE SERMON

You must be doers of the word and not only hearers who mislead
themselves. (Jas 1:22)

During a conversation with a Duke undergraduate, at a lunch
that I had paid for, I lamented that neither he nor his friends had,
in three years at the university, come to Duke Chapel to hear
my sermons. I ticked off the paybacks: "Questions? Some of my
sermons might provide answers. Lonely? Maybe you'll share the
pew with someone you could ask out next Saturday. Into classical
music? We've got a great choir." Try it, you'll be better for it.

"Aw, don't be so hard on yourself," the student counseled.
"Duke is a very selective university. These students are bright,
smart enough to know that if they got out of bed on Sunday at
an ungodly hour, sobered up, and came to the chapel, Jesus might
get mixed up in one of your sermons, mess with 'em, and make
their lives more difficult. Most of us have got enough problems on
our plate without Jesus. Can I have the rest of your fries?"

"That's the best reason I've ever heard for not listening to
a sermon," I marveled. "I'm going to do that in needlepoint,
frame it, put it over the front door of the chapel: HEY, SELF-
CENTERED, NARCISSTIC, SELF-OBSESSED DUKIES,

DON'T DARE COME INTO THIS CHURCH IF YOU DON'T WANT TO RISK HAVING JESUS ENLIST YOU!

When God's word is heard, says Karl Barth, "it is the claiming and commandeering" of the listener, not for neutral or dispassionate acquiescence to the message, but for vocation, potentially dangerous participation in Christ's mission.[1]

When Moses told what he had heard from God from the burning bush to his father-in-law, a pagan priest for some now bygone faith in Midian, then and there Jethro switched gods and began listening to Yahweh (Exod 18:18). When those who have heard, tell what they have heard to others who haven't, sometimes others hear and are changed by their hearing.

Listening occurs on the basis of what we already know. Hearing thrusts us ahead toward what we are just now learning. Lend me your ears and there's always a chance you'll come away different. Blame it on Jesus.

I ask budding preachers, "Squeamish about being complicit with God in complicating the lives of others?" Get over it.

Doers of the Word

"That was interesting," congregants at my urbane, noncommittal, university chapel congregation would say to me at the door after service. "Never thought about it that way before. I'll just have to think about that."

Translated for you non-academics: "Rather than respond to God's Word, I'll sit back and meditate on it, endlessly deferring a verdict, acting as if I've heard data rather than a demanding, divine summons."

Scripture appreciates not only the difference between merely "listening" and actually "hearing" but also the gap between hearing and doing (Ezek 33:30-32; Matt 7:24-27; Rom 2:13; Jas 1:22-25), reception of the word and the word's enactment. Deuteronomy laments our failure to "hear" surely meaning respond, do, obey (30:17). Mere "hearing" without response and obedience is castigated by Jesus (Matt 13:13). As hard as hearing can be, hearing alone isn't good enough for God (Ezek 33:30-32; Matt 7:24-27; Rom 2:13; Jas 1:22-25).

When Jesus says, "Hear, then, a parable," he means more than physically to receive sound waves in your auricles, or even intellectually to affirm an interesting idea. Reception of the Word of God entails complex, transformative human engagement. Which is to say that sermons are known by their effects, the sort of lives procured by listening.

Jesus says that those who have only the right words ("Lord, Lord . . .") unaccompanied by deeds have misunderstood (Matt 7:21). Then there's Jesus's parable of the two brothers. One had the words, "Dad, I'll be happy to do as you have asked" but remained sprawled on the couch playing video games. The other brother insolently responded to his father's request, "You can't order me around," but eventually repented and went to work (Matt 21:28-32). Think hard now, which brother pleased Dad?

When questioned about his messianic identity by, of all people, the disciples of his cousin John the Baptist, Jesus responded with evidence that he was being heard: "Go report to John what you have seen *and heard*. Those who were blind are able to see. Those who were crippled now walk. People with skin diseases are cleansed. Those who were deaf *now hear*. Those who were dead are raised up. And good news is preached to the poor" (Luke 7:22, emphasis mine).

If a church can't point every now and then to some transformative signs and wonders that God is performing through it—a few poor who heard hopeful, empowering good news, a couple of corpses risen from the dead—the world is right to wonder what's the point of preaching.

Life had taken a twist since I had known her as a Duke undergraduate:

Dear Will:

I defied my parents, just like I told you I would, and went into high school teaching. I figured that was the end of my rebellion. God had other plans.

A friend talked me into teaching a class at the Central Correctional Institution. Life-changing. So, one thing led to another and, long story short, I've quit my job with the school system, downsized to a studio apartment, sold most of what I had, and now I'm teaching four classes a week at the prison. Loving every minute.

How did I end up here? I wouldn't have known this is what God wanted out of me if it had not been for that sermon you preached in Duke Chapel about eight years ago, the one about the rich man and Jesus. You said that when Jesus told him to go, sell all he had and follow him, the man just walked away. Then you asked, "Got the guts to follow Jesus?"

That's when it clicked. I wouldn't have known a crazy God's crazy plans for me if it hadn't been for your crazy sermon.

Gratefully,

Jane[2]

Surely you lay listeners know why I keep this letter in my desk, top drawer.

In the medieval Mass, when the bell rang and the priest hoisted the sacred host, the people clambered to catch a glimpse of the priestly transposition of the bread into the Body of Christ as the priest intoned, *Hoc est corpus meum,* "This is my body." (Our "hocus-pocus," is derived from these mysterious words of magical incantation.) The priest alone concocted the presence of Christ, so it mattered little if the people understood the words or were even present.

Protestant Reformers countered that the people's reception of the sacrament was integral to Christ's real presence among the congregation. In bread and wine, and also in the gathered body of Christ, Christ was bodily present, not so much on the table as among the receiving congregation gathered about the table.

To say, "I listened to a sermon this morning," isn't saying much. Only in response is the circle of God's word complete. The Acts of the Apostles tells the history of the early church as a series of sermons in which there's a call for active response from hearers, though without guarantee (3:12-21; 13:26-33; etc.). Response is not in the hands of the preacher. Peter delivers a short, poorly illustrated sermon and three thousand people respond "What then should we do?" (Acts 2:37). Stephen preaches a well-wrought biblical sermon; listeners stone him to death (7:1-53).

"If you have ears to hear, hear!" preaches Jesus, inviting listeners to step up and take responsibility for the enactment of his message (Mark 4:9). That's why I say that you listeners have the tougher job even than preachers. You must not only hear but also figure out how to apply the word of God. After my sermon, "Serving God in Your Daily Work," a businessperson called me that night. "I want to do what you eloquently advocated in your sermon. Tomorrow morning I've got to fire five people in order to save my business and keep my loan with the bank. How can I do that as a Christian?"

Thanks for the feedback.

She made an appointment with me to talk about my preaching. "Do you have any idea how tough it is to be a public school teacher *and* a Christian at the same time?" she asked. She thereby reminded me that my job as a preacher is "to equip God's people for the work of serving and building up the body of Christ" (Eph 4:12). If your preacher isn't outfitting you for the demands of your discipleship, do all you can to get your preacher's attention. Failing at that, find another preacher.

Helping the Holy Spirit Help Us to Hear

What I've said in this book points to an experience that can be had only outside of this book. No practical handbook actually solves the problems that it addresses because problems are solved only by action. When your problem is how to get more out of sermons, a book might give some hints, some understandings that help you reframe how you listen, but nothing solves the problem of hearing a sermon like actively listening to one.

Daring to listen, curiosity, eagerness for surprise, open mindedness, willingness to receive God's revelation and then to be employed in God's work are all worthy attributes of listeners. And yet, don't worry. A dearth of these fine listener traits will not keep God from trying to speak to you in a sermon. Indifferent, unresponsive, doltish listeners are unintimidating to a God who reserves the right to speak to whomever God chooses. Think burning bush and be either warned or take heart.

A Preacher's Prayer

Lord, send me listeners who:

- *Come to a sermon hoping to hear more than mere confirmation of what they've always heard, playful listeners who enjoy surprises.*

- *Allow a sermon to speak to the person seated down the pew from them truth that they've already digested.*

- *Even if this Sunday's sermon does not become their sermon, at least they are nice enough to say on the way out, "Oh well. Wasn't our choir just great today?"*

- *Doubt their doubts, refuse to take their unbelief too seriously, willing to have their imagination stoked, funded, and fueled by scripture and a preacher who dares to connect them with an unruly ancient text.*

- *Divest themselves of that modern tendency to think that they are perfectly capable to serve as judge and jury on all truth that's uttered in church.*

- *Don't demand too easy understanding, too immediate relevance, and are willing to finish the sermon next week.*

- *Bedevil me and the Lord with, Why? How? What time is it? Was that meant for me? Who's in charge here? Is this all there is? Does God think I'm more courageous than I am?*

- *Are willing to hazard meeting the God who so very much wants to connect with them.*

- *Know that sermons are acts of risky creativity that sometimes work and sometimes don't and are therefore charitable enough afterward to say to the preacher, "So? You've had a busy week?"*

- *Expect to become more resilient, resourceful disciples by matching themselves up against a sermon.*

- *Send verbal and nonverbal feedback to the preacher to show that they are listening.*

- *Clear away distractions, silence phones, focus attention, and make eye contact, acting as if they are the listener that I hope they'll be.*

- *Don't mind, maybe even yearn for, being born again, then again and again.*

- *If I venture confession of my own doubts or struggles, respond, "Me too."*

Lord, if you send me listeners like these, I promise to begin work on my sermon sooner than Saturday. (Okay, you don't have to tell me that last Sunday's wasn't my best effort, I already knew that.)

Send me the listeners I crave and, so help me God, my sermons will become encouragement for conversation with you. Amen.

And as for you resolutely unresponsive listeners, be advised that in even the worst of sermons badly delivered by the crummiest of preachers, God may speak. Though we are only receptors, receivers in the divine-human colloquy, never the initiators or sustainers, scripture says that God will figure out a way to address us and enable us to hear: "What do you have that you didn't receive? And if you received it, then why are you bragging as if you didn't receive it?" (1 Cor 4:7). Gift—unsought, unearned, undeserved.

A bishop preached on the parable of the Sower urging us to be "good soil, well cultivated to hear the word of God." We were directed to engage in more serious Bible study, do homework before coming to church, stir up sympathy with the plight of preachers, get a better attitude, sit up straight, pay attention, and keep our hands to ourselves. While it's fun to ponder the bishop's comparison of Methodists to mud, the sermon was a misrepresentation of the parable. Surely Jesus's story is of the miraculous fruitfulness of God's word, not a moralistic exhortation for us to become a better class of dirt. We so want to believe that the God-human colloquy is up to us. Self-salvation is always more popular than falling into the hands of a dying, rising, and revealing God.

The word of God is heard by making itself heard, says Karl Barth. "The possibility of knowing the word of God is God's miracle on us,"[3] which we can receive but never produce. What did Moses do to be addressed from the burning bush? How did the Israelites earn life-sustaining manna in the wilderness (Exod 16)? Good news: When it comes to receiving a sermon, it's not all up to you. The bad news? It's not up to you.

Still, the odds of your hearing and responding to a sermon are good because of the God we've got. Jesus was crucified in a vain attempt to shut him up. Yet in every culture, in all times and places, Christ has risen up and spoken for himself and had his say. Nobody has ever created a culture so hostile, an intellectual defense so solid, a political system so godless, clergy so corrupt and doltish, a sermon so narcotic that it keeps Jesus from sneaking in, kicking open a locked door, igniting a fire, speaking up, and speaking out as he pleases. From the first, Jesus went where he was not sought and showed up to people who didn't ask to meet him, engaging in conversation with those who would have been happy left alone.

"I've had a hellish week," she said to me after service.

"I'm sorry to hear that," I unctuously responded.

"My son is drinking again. New boss doesn't like me, so I'm under the gun at work. On top of that I've had some problems with depression. So, I came here this morning needing to hear some comfort and consolation," she said.

"I hope my sermon was helpful."

"Not particularly. I came here for comfort and care only to have Jesus give me an assignment!"

I double-dog dare you; keep listening.

Chapter 7

HEARING AID

He rolled up the scroll, gave it back to the synagogue assistant,
and sat down. Every eye in the synagogue was fixed on him.
He began to explain to them, "Today, this scripture has been
fulfilled just as you heard it." (Luke 4:20-21)

A Broadway actor told me that the highlight of her nightly
preparation for going on stage was to peer through the curtain
and watch the audience assembling. "The anticipation and ex-
pectancy on their faces gave me what I needed to give 'em my
best," she said. Her comment helped me see that the time before
the service, in which I roamed the sanctuary greeting worshipers,
was one of the most important steps in my sermon preparation.
Standing on the front steps of Duke Chapel and watching people
streaming in the front door on the Sunday after 9/11, the fear on
their faces, gave me the nerve to stand and deliver a sermon (on
Gen 1) that I could not have preached without their help.

"My son goes in for brain surgery tomorrow morning," she
said as I welcomed her to worship. "So, I look forward to your
sermon."

Come on, Holy Spirit, don't let me stumble. Line?

In a self-help, mother-I'd-rather-do-it-myself culture, it's risky
to give guidance about how to listen to preaching. Listening for
God is a human activity; hearing God can only be done with help

from God. Still, God has determined you to be a conversation partner. Preaching is too important to be left to preachers. Speakers for God need all the help you hearers and doers of the Word of God can give.

How Can You Help?

Pray! Begin contact with God before your preacher makes contact with you. You are about to enter what could be a very difficult conversation. Pray the Prayer for Illumination, "Open our hearts and minds . . ." with particular fervor. Beseeching God to "open my ears," auto-suggestion whereby you put yourself in a teachable frame of mind or miraculous work of the Holy Spirit? *Yes.*

Listen for the preacher to give you signals, help in listening. "What I'm trying to say . . . " "To put it simply . . ." "My main point is . . ." Note the preacher's posture, eye contact, and gestures as well as tone of voice. When a preacher leans toward you over the pulpit, brace yourself. You're about to be jabbed by the main point. What do you suspect is the preacher's emotional investment behind the words of the sermon? How is the preacher attempting to signal those aspects of the sermon that the preacher most earnestly wants you to hear?

Read the biblical text for the sermon beforehand, even if it's just scanning it briefly. A benefit of having a preacher who uses the Revised Common Lectionary as a source for sermon texts is that individuals and groups in the congregation can do in-depth study of texts. I know a small group who, on Wednesday nights, studies the lectionary texts for the upcoming Sunday, always ending their meetings by asking, "If you were the preacher, which of the assigned lessons would you preach and what would be your theme?"

Go ahead, speculate on the problem for which this sermon is the solution. Guess why the preacher has been compelled by the text and the congregational context to say these things in this way at this time. What's the "itch" for which the sermon is the scratch, the question that's answered by the sermon?

If a title is given, speculate on where the preacher might go. Some newsworthy event from the past week, a debate occurring within the congregation, may build your anticipation.

Regular listeners to a pastor's sermons have the advantage of having heard this person speak. They know when the preacher is in danger of falling off the wagon on the trip between text and sermon. They pick up mannerisms, cues, habits of speech, know which biblical texts or social issues fascinate or bore the speaker, which themes preoccupy the preacher, and can predict when a sermon will take a certain turn.

I once served as an associate to a senior pastor who would habitually end sermons, "Therefore, we must go forth as Christ's ambassadors, his chosen representatives, those who have been commissioned to . . ." Hearing "ambassadors . . . representatives" the congregation became Pavlov's dog. From my perch behind the pastor I watched them gather their coats and hats, thinking, "Well, we're about done here."

During the pandemic I regularly watched a noted preacher who, no matter the biblical text, predictably ended sermons with the litany, "to struggle against racism, sexism, and economic exploitation . . ." Tagging each sermon with these slogans indicating self-identification as a presumed prophet was more important to the preacher than listening to the text or speaking to the congregational context. If I just say the words, I will have done something. Sort of.

Expect to be surprised. We preachers sometimes reassure ourselves with the thought, "My people don't like hearing controversial ideas from the pulpit." Check that out. "I'll admit that few of us come to church on Sunday morning hoping to be jostled and jolted," a layperson said, "but if there's one thing that we fear more than being offended by a sermon it's being *bored out of our minds!*"[1]

People-pleasing preachers need lay encouragement to try to please God more than our listeners.

I tell seminarians, when studying a biblical text as a source for a sermon, "Look for the trouble."[2] What about the text is confusing, dissonant, or conflicted? "Trouble" can be the preacher's friend. A favorite sermon form is the old "Problem-Solution" format. Set up some problem early in the sermon, then spend the rest of the sermon resolving or at least reframing the problem. Restating solutions that everyone already knows isn't interesting; posing questions, problems, and dilemmas and then offering surprising resolutions stirs engagement.

Don't show up at church expecting to hear confirmation of what you've always believed. Note the "new" in Good News. Sometimes preaching lessens the gap between us and God and at other times that chasm is widened as you are made uneasy by hearing from a God whose ways are not our ways, whose thoughts are not ours (Isa 55:8).

Most of us are fearful to let go of our accustomed ways of seeing things. While listening to a sermon, loosen your grip just a bit on what you know in the expectation that you may be given the gift of new insight or fresh understanding.

The gospel is often the bad news about something taken from you before it is good news of a gift given to you. Jesus compared God's work to that of a thief who breaks in at night and rips off your stuff (Matt 24:43). Luther likened the sermon to a surgeon's scalpel.[3] Sometimes a sermon gives you a novel way of thinking about things. But let's be honest; occasionally there is loss—the defeat of cherished prejudice, the demise of inherited, childish ideas of the faith, the disruption of a placid life. God the thief has found a way to case the joint, sneak in unawares, when your guard is down, and rip off accumulations that you thought you couldn't live without. In your journey with God, expect bumps along the way.

The response, "I've never heard anything like that before," is revealing. There's a good chance that the respondent has been led to believe that being Christian is equivalent to being a thinking, caring, middle-class American and therefore is surprised to be surprised. The person thinks that we get to be Christian, not by hearing Good News that converts us but by drinking the water and breathing the air and living in a nice part of town. Christian is the normal, conventional, American thing to do. To be troubled or jolted by a sermon is therefore an offense against my presumption that I'm a Christian by virtue of being lucky enough to be born in the USA.

I'm hoping that you will agree that your church today is in a missional context in which growing numbers of North American Christians are feeling like missionaries in the culture we once thought we owned. The Christian way is no longer the American way, if it ever was.[4] Vast numbers of people are clueless about biblical language, stories, or worldview. In short, we find ourselves in a cultural situation akin to the New Testament when Christianity preached its way into a world that was not Christian. When nine-out-of-ten Americans say "God" it's doubtful they mean the one who lived briefly, died violently, and rose unexpectedly. In a missionary context, if you are listening to a preacher who is attempting to be faithful to scripture and orthodox faith, there are bound to be bumps as the one being evangelized, the pagan surprised by the message of the missionary is *you*.

If it's true that there's much controversy, disunity, and contention among Americans these days, I could make a case that the church is the optimum location for consideration of contentious subjects. Speakers on the floor of Congress or in a college classroom don't have the blessing of standing up and saying, "Hello. I'm a sinner as are all of you, so we're all liable to error and falsehood, all in danger of myopic vision and pigheadedness, yet all of us have been assembled by Jesus to put up with one another in the church, to grow closer toward Christ together, and to receive Christ from one another. Now, let's talk. And after we argue and fight, whether we disagree or agree, together let's go to the Lord's Table."

When a church fears disunion and division more than it fears failure to preach the gospel truth, uninteresting sermons are unavoidable. It's too much for you to expect your preacher to testify to the truth of Jesus Christ without possible refusal by some listeners. Surely, I'm not the only Christian who doesn't enjoy having my biases and self-deceits exposed and named in a sermon. And yet I know I wouldn't be as close to what Christ wants out of me if not for risky sermons by courageous preachers who dared say what they said to me in a sermon because Jesus put them up to it.

I'm all for unity and comity within a congregation. However, Christ gives listeners the freedom not to listen, even to walk away when they hear more than they can take. (They won't have to walk far to find a church where nothing new or challenging is uttered from the pulpit.) Sometimes their withdrawal signifies not a failure to reach them but a validation that the congregation has indeed become a place where the truth of Christ is told in spite of the cost, a church that's willing to be the body of Christ in motion rather than settle for being a warmhearted club to keep older adults out of trouble.

"Well, I hope they find what they're looking for," I said to a lay leader in one of my churches after a couple stormed out in a huff.

"Wherever they land, it won't take them long to be dissatisfied," said the layperson. "Then they'll have to go through this all over again. I don't think they're as fragile as they think, but maybe they know their limits. Still, I worry. It ain't that easy to find a church where you're safe from Jesus."

Paul was big on congregational unity, constantly urging congregations to agree with one another and live together in love. Still, Paul acknowledges that division within a congregation can be a necessary by-product of truthful preaching. Unity and togetherness are not the church's sole concern (1 Cor 11:18).

You may not be the best listener in the world, but if you have not yet murdered a preacher, for any of your faults, you are more charitable and open-minded than many auditors in the Bible (Luke 4:28-30; Mark 6:14-27; Acts 7:54-60; etc.).

Ask questions. If you don't know a term that's used in the sermon, ask the preacher. (Your request for a definition may embarrass, revealing that the preacher doesn't know either.) Perhaps your preacher will enjoy pointing you toward resources for better understanding. Your question may also be a polite way of reminding your preacher not to throw out words like "eschatology." Nobody likes a show-off.

Patience! An episode in Jesus's preaching is instructive: "With many such parables he continued to give them the word, *as much as they were able to hear*" (Matt 13:33, emphasis mine). Sometimes Jesus lovingly holds back, awaiting a more propitious time until we are "able to hear." Paul brags that he fed his new church baby food until they could handle more substantial nourishment (1 Cor 3:2). There was a four-hundred-year hiatus in the conversation between God and the Hebrew children until the bush that talked. It must have taken thirty years and a dozen sermons before the penny dropped and the virginal conception of Jesus in Mary's womb made sense to me. Some biblical truth stretches you; patiently await the moment when you receive the faith you previously lacked.

"He spoke to them only in parables, then *explained everything to his disciples when he was alone with them*" (Matt 13:34, emphasis mine). Sometimes a sermon is best understood by sitting down with your pastor for a one-on-one. Harry Emerson Fosdick said that "one of the best tests of a sermon is the number of people afterward who wish to see the preacher alone."[5]

When you say, "I didn't get anything out of that sermon," that could be a commentary, not on your lack of intellect but on your dearth of preparation for listening. If you hear, that means that by God's grace—working through faithful parents, good Christian education, friendship with the friends of God, a college religion class, dogged persistence in Bible reading, tenacious church attendance, reading this book—you've had more put into you, so you get more out of the sermon.

You say, "I didn't get anything out of that sermon." I say, don't be so sure. Sermons work on listeners at different times and places than when and where they were delivered. The gospel is truth that can come to you in an instant and yet take a lifetime fully to receive. For instance, I don't know anyone who says, "This is what I believe about same-sex unions" who believes exactly what they thought just ten years ago. The first name for the church was "The Way." All of us, not where we once were, theologically speaking, all of us on the way with Jesus somewhere else.

Much of our listening is aspirational. In listening, sometimes you are practicing faith before you completely have it. To hit a good golf shot, you must first put yourself in position, place your feet right, be conscious of your backswing, visualize, prepare your body, imagine yourself hitting the perfect shot. Now swing. That's you, imagining on the way to believing.

Anne Lamott, in her memoir *Traveling Mercies*, says that when she first attended the forlorn Presbyterian church in her neighborhood, the sermon sounded like "talk about Martians."[6] Yet she came back next Sunday.

Months later, one evening when her defenses were down and she was in a drunken stupor, Jesus nabbed her. While Lamott's life-changing encounter with Christ occurred at home rather than in church and not as a direct result of a sermon, Lamott is clear that the sermons she heard—few specifics of which she remembers—left her vulnerable to the overtures of Jesus.

"It took us a year before we figured out how to listen to your preaching," one of my church members confessed. "Your brain works weird. Aren't you glad we didn't give up?"

Don't demand that your pastor capture and keep your attention throughout the whole sermon. It's okay for your mind to wander. We listen faster than people speak, so congregations are always scampering ahead of their preachers, positioning themselves where they think the sermon is headed, leaving the preacher in a cloud of dust as the pedestrian preacher plods along with, "Let me repeat again what I said earlier . . ."

A good illustration or story is an invitation to check out of the sermon and go romp about in the playground of your imagination. A casual reference may set off an explosion of memory that will require you to step aside for a moment and relish.

What you experience as distraction can be the Holy Spirit working on you to show you something even more relevant and interesting than what the preacher had in mind. Perhaps you are preoccupied with refashioning and refitting the sermon for your personal application. Your itinerant mind could be a sign that the sermon is doing its intended work.

As a preacher I've got to be open to the possibility that when a listener fails to receive the word I have so energetically preached, perhaps lack of hearing is not due to the listener's limitations but to a gracious God's defense of God's people from falsehood and error. When I recall some of the youthfully self-righteous, judgmental sermons I preached in my first years of ministry, I take heart that some of my listeners were able to say, "Son, you got a lot to learn," tossing my precious sermon in the bin on their way to Sunday dinner.

Talk back.[7] In a one-on-one conversation, listener response is immediate. Feedback on a sermon takes more time and must be more intentional. Your preacher can't receive feedback if you don't speak up. Speak to your preacher as your preacher tries to speak to you, speaking in a way that might be heard:

"I was interested that you said . . ."

"I'd like to hear more about . . ."

"If what you said about that text is true, that makes me wonder . . . ?"

"Thanks for tackling a difficult subject. I bet that wasn't easy."

"While I'm not sure I agree with you, I'm grateful that you prepare so well and that you don't back off from grappling with tough issues."

Before saying "I disagree," ask yourself, "Even in my disagreement, how has this sermon stoked my imagination and got me to thinking, associating, and remembering?"

Be critical. As a listener, your first task is to try to hear a sermon; your second job is to criticize it. I hope that your criticism will be thoughtful and charitable, well-meaning and appreciative; still, the preacher wants to say something to you, so why should you not be the valued critic? Both positive and negative criticism are sure signs that sermons are being heard. Critical feedback is about the only way preachers get better.

In your response, say more than what you like or dislike; say what's helpful or unhelpful about the sermon and why. There is a real difference here. Who can disagree with a person's likes or dislikes? Personal taste is unchallengeable; critical appraisals can be contested or supported.[8] As an appreciative critic, appeal to the biblical text that has been preached, to other biblical texts that contradict what was preached, to church teaching and doctrine, before putting forth your personal feelings.

"Why don't you preach more about the Holy Spirit?" he asked.

"Do you know what it's like to be nineteen, make a promise to yourself, and then break it?" There was pathos in her voice.

"You speak so glibly of God speaking to you. God's never said anything to me."

My preaching was forever changed by these listener responses I can't get out of my head. Every time I sit down to prepare a sermon, listeners who cared enough about me and my preaching to talk back crowd into my study and make me a better preacher.

Beware: Every preacher remembers negative comments from listeners long after we've heard them and forgets affirmative responses soon after they are uttered. Thoughtful listeners are stewards of adverse comeback, knowing pastors' tendencies to magnify negative pushback. In offering feedback, your goal is to help your preacher become a better listener to you and to the biblical text, not to muzzle your preacher with constant, carping complaining.

As a preacher (that is, as a critical listener to preaching) I know there's a risk that by becoming a more reflective listener, always analyzing and critiquing, the delight of the mystery of one human being arising and telling others the truth of God is diminished. The wonder of preaching wilts under the paralysis of analysis. As you become a more critical listener, I pray that your appreciation for preaching doesn't dissipate but deepens.

Don't expect every sermon to be helpful. Some sermons must be listened to with charity but then resolutely forgotten. Assume that the sermon targeted another listener; hope that your neighbor got something out of it. As for you, there's always next Sunday.

When you read a book, it has gone through a complex vetting process. An editor has said (as has been said often to me), "In this paragraph, I have no idea what you are talking about. Rewrite."

But a sermon is usually the product of one set of hands. David Letterman had a dozen writers help him come up with a short nightly monologue; a preacher is backed up only by a couple of turgid biblical commentaries. The president may prepare a few speeches a month; a preacher is up at bat every Sunday.

It's some help that most churches vet preachers and have educational requirements for them, but this is no sure defense against bad sermons. As you listen, "test the spirits" (1 John 4:1). Scripture interprets scripture and tests its interpretation. Some sermons, no matter how well intended, just don't chin up to the biblical bar.

In responding, "I understand what you said" must precede "I disagree" or "You are wrong." Before disposing of a sermon that you've just heard, ask yourself: Have I simply dismissed this sermon because it's too challenging to my preconceptions? Has the sermon sailed over my head because the preacher was attempting to say something beyond the preacher's powers of statement? Is this sermon requiring too much of me? Has my lack of biblical knowledge left me ill-equipped for so biblical a sermon?

Talk back, but let your resistance be appropriate to the nature of a sermon. To say, "I do not like your sermon because it challenges my experience as a white male over fifty," is shallow. Who cares if you say, "That's not what I was brought up to believe"? Tell me that my sermon contradicts scripture or that I distorted the biblical text; now you're talking. Let me hear more.

Some preachers provide blank space in the Sunday bulletin, telling hearers, "Write down the major insights you received in today's sermon." I don't care for the encouragement of note taking during the sermon. As I said, my own experience with listener feedback taught me that a sermon is much more than an elucidation of abstract propositions or dogmatic assertions. A good sermon stirs the imagination, sometimes with emotions too deep for words. A sermon "works" not simply when it is comprehended by the listener but when the listener is encountered by the risen Christ. Such encounters are too big for notation on the back of a bulletin. Besides, while you are writing down notes from the sermon, you may be missing important visual cues from the preacher and congregation that would have augmented your experience of the sermon.

As you exit a film, your friend asks, "What did you get out of the movie?" Sometimes you are able to say, "I really liked what she said when she lost her dog."

But sometimes you are at a loss for words, annoyed by the question, not because you didn't get anything out of the movie but because the movie got you. Good sermons are often just like that.

Encourage. Your goal is to help your preacher help your discipleship. You know from your own experience that asking questions of someone is better received than outright criticism. Offer insights. Want to hear another sermon like the one you just heard? Praise the preacher.

Some laity, because of their work responsibilities and community service, have more extensive public speaking experience than their pastor. When I marveled at the sermon insights of one of the businesspersons in my congregation, she said, "I don't run a real estate company; I talk people into giving me money. Say to someone, 'Give me ten thousand dollars,' you better be good at speaking on your feet."

"Teach me to do that," I said.

Assist. Help your pastor find the time to devote to good preaching. Because of the difficulty and invisibility of sermon preparation, it's easy for pastors to allow a host of other pastoral duties to crowd the schedule. So they phone it in, put it on cruise control, and call it a sermon.

My first week as pastor in a declining urban congregation, I met with the Pastor-Parish Relations Committee. "If you don't help me set priorities for myself, I'm going to do what I did in my last congregation; it worked there and besides, it's what I know how to do. Tell me what is most important for me to do here."

I had written down on notecards twenty or so duties that I might perform in a given week, everything from visiting the sick to overseeing finances. I said to them, "I want you to take these cards and rank my tasks." I left the room. Twenty minutes later they called me back. I was surprised that of all my responsibilities, at the top they ranked "Preaching."

"With our shrinking membership, I thought you might have ranked number one as 'Visiting Prospective Members,'" I said.

"You are new in this town. Who do you know? It's our job to reach out in the community; it's your job to offer a sermon that's worth inviting someone to hear."

I need to get out of this meeting and get to work on next Sunday's homily.

"Do you know how much time it takes to come up with an interesting sermon?" I persisted.

"We thought you just got them by mail from Nashville," someone chortled.

Cute.

I walked them through the study, prayer, deliberation, and meditation required to produce a sermon.

"Take the time you need to make preaching your priority, and we'll back you up if the congregation asks, 'What does our new preacher do with his time?' Show us that you think we are worthy of the best sermons you can preach."

Thanks for helping me keep the main thing the main thing.

Find ways to show your preacher that you value and need a good sermon. Maybe this sounds crazy to laypeople, but we preachers need to be reminded that preaching is the most important service that we render to a congregation.

God calls the whole church to proclaim the gospel. The preacher's job is to equip the saints in church on Sunday so they can preach to the world Monday through Saturday (Eph 4:11). When you're listening to a sermon, you are listening not simply for a word on how to live a more abundant life (everybody already does that). You listen as part of your baptismal responsibility. Some of the baptized preach to a children's Sunday school class, others whisper the gospel through prison bars while visiting the incarcerated, another responds to a coworker who leans over a computer keyboard and casually asks, "You really believe all that stuff?"

Help your preacher help you know what to say when it's your turn to preach.

The month I became bishop in Alabama, I met with Ms. Mattie Battle, legendary president of the United Methodist Women. During our conversation I asked her how I could lead the North Alabama Conference forward.

"Bishop, you have got to do a better job of evaluating and equipping our preachers. When I was an educator, I was evaluated every year by my principal, my colleagues, even by my students.

I then set goals for improvement. Preachers are nobody special. They can grow too."

"I promise that we'll devise a way for our preachers to receive evaluation so they can set goals for strengthening their preaching," I said.

Then Ms. Battle took my hand and said, "Bishop, you are new here. But let me tell you. It's hard being black in Alabama without good preaching. Our Methodists require the very best preaching the church has to offer."[9]

Preaching became my top episcopal priority. I preached nearly every Sunday in at least one of our churches. I also vowed that I would not appoint a pastor whom I had not heard preach. Every January and February I listened to recordings of sermons by pastors who were up for a move. Then I sent written responses to each as my attempt to bolster their ministry of preaching.

In my memoir, *Accidental Preacher*, I wrote:

> Some congregations get the preaching they deserve. We preachers form a congregation through our sermons, but congregations also form us. One morning I opened a small, powder blue envelope addressed with a flowery hand that I knew to be that of one of our older women at Duke Chapel. Folded within the note was a newspaper clipping that reported American troops had buried alive a score of Iraqi soldiers in their trenches during a battle.
>
> "By the time we got there, nothing but arms and hands sticking out of the sand," said one GI.
>
> "Did you preach on this?" she asked in her note. "I don't get out much anymore, but I listen to your sermons on television and I don't recall that you mentioned this atrocity. Please! Where is the moral voice of our clergy? We are frighteningly dependent upon our preachers."
>
> With your help, Alice Philips, one day I might become a faithful preacher.[10]

Allow your preacher to fail. Sometimes a sermonic dud ("I couldn't understand the sermon") becomes, in time, a winner ("Wow. The Christian faith is more fascinating than I had imagined"). And yet, even Tiger Woods is permitted a bogey now and then.

In asking your preacher not to be boring, you are requesting creativity. Sometimes the creator's intentions aren't realized. A preacher who has never failed has never dared.

As a bold preacher ascends the heights of some difficult-to-reach biblical text, the preacher may slip. Praise your preacher for chutzpah (a trait too often lacking in clergy) and urge an attempt at another ascent, but maybe not next Sunday.

When an arrow hits the bulls-eye, it misses most of the target. Sometimes what was, in your hearing, a communicative flop was a pastoral care success for another.

I preached at a youth conference on the assigned theme, "Valuing Families." I noted few happy families in scripture, particularly Jesus's own family who thought he was nuts (Mark 3:20-21). I surmised that Jesus had a more expansive definition of our true family than the family you were born into, that Jesus calls us, by our baptism, to come be part of a more resourceful, expansive, diverse family named "church."

After my sermon some of the adult organizers lined up to complain: "You didn't speak to the theme we gave you" and "You shouldn't criticize parents in front of teenagers."

After the grown-ups had their harrumph, then came the youth: "Cool sermon. I didn't know God had any other plans for me than to be the success that my parents wanted."

"When my folks went through a divorce, my life went to hell. But now I realize that my church—which I love, by the way—is the family God wanted me to have all along."

Sermons that fail to be what you needed at the moment are sometimes tucked away until you need them in the worst sort of way. For instance, when you attend a funeral you likely overhear a sermon that is directed at those who are in acute grief. File that sermon for later retrieval when it's your turn to be visited by death.

As you go about your week, try out what you have heard in last Sunday's sermon. Perhaps it fits better than you first thought. Who knows? Maybe you are a more courageous disciple than you presupposed.

The preacher has not been given the ability to judge when people have heard and when they have not. Sometimes, when we get an angry reaction from a hearer of a sermon, the anger is not the result of our having stated the gospel poorly but of testifying so clearly. When someone comes out muttering, "I just don't understand," maybe they have truly understood.

It's possible to hear a sermon in real time, as a momentous, life-changing present event. More often, sermons' effects are cumulative, incremental, Sunday after Sunday, as one thing connects with another, and our ears are gradually opened to receive truth that made no impact when first heard. Be prepared to sit through lots of sermons. Preaching doesn't just want to inform, it wants to form, reform your consciousness, fund and fuel your imagination. That takes time.

Say to me, "Your sermon was irrelevant to me and my needs," and I'll respond, "Not relevant *yet*." God's got ways. All the time in the world.

As Paul said of his own preaching, "I planted, Apollos watered, but God made it grow . . . I laid a foundation like a wise master builder according to God's grace that was given to me, but someone else is building on top of it" (1 Cor 3:6, 10). The sermon that failed to mean anything to you at the time is discovered, post-sermon, to be a seed that was planted.

A woman recently said to me, "Today I finally ended a sermon that you left unfinished twenty years ago."

Try to love the preacher you've got rather than the one you think you ought to have. Preachers age, get better with experience, or run out of steam with the accumulation of Sundays. Try to enjoy your preacher at your preacher's time of life. A young preacher can be like listening to your smart-mouthed grandson who, by saying things that you wish he wouldn't, keeps you young.

Bessie Parker, step-grandmother of my wife, Patsy, was South Carolina Methodism's first ordained woman. In the 1950s, Bessie blew through dozens of Methodist churches with her snow-white hair and clerical collar, playing her everybody's-stereotypical-grandmother routine for all it's worth. Listener response to Bessie's sermons proved the irresistibility of grandmotherly wisdom. God can use the age and stage of your preacher to your advantage.

Some are better preachers than pastors. I'm all for a doctor having good bedside manner, but what I want most in my surgeon is competence, even if he or she is short on personality. Caring, available pastors are a dime a dozen. Excellent preachers who care enough not to care about your hurt feelings are not.

Others are better pastors than preachers. Even though your beloved pastor may have difficulty mastering the complexities of pulpit communication, you can be sure that what's being said from the pulpit, however poorly, is intended for your good. Trust

God to have called your pastor into the ministry with the best of intentions.

Don't give up. Keep showing up, doggedly, daringly persistent in your expectation that eventually God will dare to prompt your pastor to dare to speak for God to you. Jesus doesn't let your refusal to hear stump him. The risen Christ is able, even eager, to go where uninvited (John 20:19ff.). You come to church in the wrong frame of mind, not particularly wanting or expecting to hear God. Don't worry. Christ is free to address whomever he chooses. The word of God makes its way in the world in spite of the world's repeated refusals. Christ loves to surprise.

Timing not good for you to be in conversation with a living, demanding God? At a point in your life when you have got enough challenges on your plate and are not looking for more hassles? Your schedule is overbooked, and you are burdened with cares so you're not out looking for new assignments?

God doesn't care. The "Spirit blows where it will" (John 3:8) descending upon and working through preachers, listeners ready or not. Mulish listeners are God's self-assignment. God will speak to you if God wills and the poor, old, dull church, for all its faults, becomes holy ground where daring truth is told and just as daringly received, even by the likes of us.

And In Conclusion

Then there's the one about the young listener who was bored to death by one of Saint Paul's sermons, Eutychus (whose name ironically means "Lucky," Acts 20:7-12). While Paul went on and on, missing a number of good stopping places in his sermon that night, Eutychus, who had perched himself in a window so he could keep an eye on more interesting activity in the street, unluckily fell out the window to his death below.

"Myrtle, go to the piano and lead folks in 'Rock of Ages,'" sighs an aggravated Paul as he interrupts his sermon and goes down to the street. There, he raises Eutychus from the dead, giving him a short exhortation on Sermon Listening Safety. Returning to the regathered congregation, Paul continues: "Let's see, where was I before I was so rudely interrupted by an irresponsible youth who wouldn't have such a bad headache if he had been paying attention to my sermon?"

If Paul is patron saint of us preachers, Eutychus ought to be the darling of you listeners. Even if you sometimes sleep through sermons, Christ promises to jerk you awake, land you on your head, and raise you from the dead so that the conversation between you and God can continue. Your somnambulism doesn't stump a relentlessly revealing God.

I could go on. But I don't want to be one of those preachers who goes on and on, missing good stopping places, adding, qualifying, reiterating, and recapping because they're insecure about God's ability to make a sermon work.

As Luther concluded many of his sermons: "That's enough for today." I can end, knowing that I'll not have the last word between you and God. This book, like next Sunday's sermon, is whatever God makes of it.

Thanks for daring to listen.

ABOUT THE AUTHOR

Will Willimon is a preacher and teacher of preachers. He is a United Methodist bishop (retired) and serves as professor of the practice of christian ministry and director of the Doctor of Ministry program at Duke Divinity School, Durham, North Carolina. For twenty years he was Dean of the Chapel at Duke University. A 1996 Baylor University study named him among the twelve most effective preachers in the English-speaking world. The Pew Research Center found that Willimon was one of the most widely read authors among Protestant clergy in 2005. His quarterly *Pulpit Resource* is used by thousands of pastors throughout North America, Canada, and Australia. In 2021 he gave the prestigious Lyman Beecher Lectures on Preaching at Yale Divinity School. Those lectures became the book *Preachers Dare: Speaking for God*, which is the inspiration for his ninetieth book, *Listeners Dare: Hearing God in the Sermon*.

NOTES

Introduction

1. Gallup reported that 118 million people listened to a sermon last week. Even though researchers Kirk Hadaway and Penny Marler thought half of them were exaggerating, that's a lot of listening. See C. Kirk Hadaway and P. L. Marler, "Did You Really Go to Church This Week?: Behind the Poll Data," in *The Christian Century*, May 6, 1998, http://www.religion-online.org/showarticle.asp?title=237.

2. "Choosing a New Church or House of Worship," *Pew Research Center*, August 23, 2016, https://www.pewforum.org/2016/08/23/choosing-a-new-church-or-house-of-worship/.

3. Will Willimon, *Preachers Dare: Speaking for God* (Nashville: Abingdon, 2021).

4. Mortimer J. Adler and Charles Van Doren, *How to Read a Book*, rev. ed. (New York: Simon and Schuster, 1972).

5. Thanks to listeners Carter Rief, Grant Wacker, Jeremy Begbie, Stephen Chapman, Ann Hall, Stanley Hauerwas, Harriet Putman, Patsy Willimon, and Paul Franklyn for their help with this book.

1. God in Conversation

1. Will Willimon, *Stories* (Nashville: Abingdon, 2020), 7–8.

2. The theologian Karl Barth says that God created us to listen "for His own Word." Humanity was made for no grander purpose than listening to preaching! See Karl Barth, *Church Dogmatics: The Doctrine of the Word of God*, vol II, part 2, ed. G. W. Bromiley and

T. F. Torrance (Edinburgh: T & T Clark, 1936; English translation, 1975), 176. The first thesis of the Barmen Declaration (the statement that Barth wrote for the Confessing Church's resistance to Hitler) says: "Jesus Christ, as he is attested to us in Holy Scripture, is the one Word of God whom *we have to hear*, and whom we have to trust and obey in life and in death" (emphasis mine). It's conventional to think of the Declaration as an assertion of the freedom of preaching. Now I see that it was a declaration of the church's defiant hearing.

3. Barth says that the first thing the creature owes the Creator is silence "for the sake of hearing" and "of obeying." Karl Barth, *Church Dogmatics*, IV/4, 184.

4. Some of the following material is from Will Willimon, *God Turned Toward Us: The ABCs of Christian Faith* (Nashville: Abingdon, 2021).

5. As a professor, I get paid to listen to students, and students are coerced into listening to me. Preachers must win a hearing, which accounts for why preachers, for all their many faults, tend to be better oral communicators than professors are.

6. Dietrich Bonhoeffer, *Life Together*, trans. John W. Doberstein (San Francisco: HarperSanFrancisco, 1954), 75–76.

2. What's a Sermon For?

1. Augustine, *On Christian Doctrine*, J. F. Shaw, trans. (Mineola, NY: Dover Publications, Inc.), 27.

2. Thomas G. Long, *The Witness of Preaching* (Louisville, KY: Westminster/John Knox, 1989), 131.

3. The documentary, *A Will to Preach*, shows me moving from a biblical text to a congregational context in a sermon. See Scott Galloway, dir., *A Will to Preach* (2021, United States, Susie Films), https://www.scetv.org/watch/will-preach.

4. By exegesis I mean the preacher's careful, prayerful, open-minded listening to a biblical text.

5. By hermeneutical, I mean the interpretation of what has been heard from a biblical text, so that listeners might also hear.

6. Much of the current "attendance recession" is either a wide-

spread listener protest or a sign that listeners have heard nothing that brings them back to church.

3. Preachers Listening

1. Tom Long, as cited by Roger E. Van Harn, *Pew Rights: For People Who Listen to Sermons* (Grand Rapids, MI: Eerdmans, 1992), 28. Preachers engage in what Leander Keck called "priestly listening," listening not individually but officially, as representatives of the church. See Leander E. Keck, *The Bible in the Pulpit* (Nashville: Abingdon, 1978), 61.

2. Here I'm building on the insights of Mark Allan Powell, *What Do They Hear?* (Nashville: Abingdon, 2007), 97.

3. Theologian David Bentley Hart accused the modern world of "willful spiritual deafness" in which even "nature [much less God or Scripture] cannot speak unless spoken to, and then her answers must be only yes, no, or obedient silence. She cannot address us. . . . And we certainly cannot hear whatever voice might attempt to speak to us through her." *The Experience of God: Being, Consciousness, Bliss* (New Haven: Yale University Press, 2013), 312.

4. Saint Augustine, *On Christian Doctrine*, trans. D. W. Robertson Jr. (Indianapolis: Bobbs-Merrill, 1958), 142.

5. John Stott, an Anglican theologian, said that preachers are "called to the difficult and even painful task of 'double listening.' That is, we are to listen carefully (although of course with differing degrees of respect) both to the ancient Word and to the modern world, in order to relate the one to the other with a combination of fidelity and sensitivity." Stott defined "double listening" as "[listening to] the voice of God through Scripture and the voices of men and women around us. These voices will often contradict one another, but our purpose in listening to them both is to discover how they relate to each other." See John Stott, *The Contemporary Christian: Applying God's Word to Today's World* (Downers Grove, IL: InterVarsity Press, 1992), 13.

6. Phillips Brooks, *Lectures on Preaching* (New York: E. P. Dutton & Company, 1907), 180.

7. Jesus, that's who.

8. Brooks, *Lectures on Preaching*, 13.

9. T. S. Eliot, "East Coker," *The Complete Poems and Plays* (London: Faber, 1969), 182.

10. Willimon, *God Turned Toward Us*, 9.

4. Listeners to the Sermon

1. Quoted by Barth, *Church Dogmatics*, I, 1, 123.

2. Quoted by Barth, *Church Dogmatics*, I, 1, 135. Reformer John Calvin said that the true church is where "the Word of God [is] purely preached *and heard . . .*" (Calvin, *Institutes*, 4.1.9, emphasis mine).

3. Luther quoted by Richard Lischer in *A Theology of Preaching* (Nashville: Abingdon, 1981), 70.

4. Karl Barth, *Church Dogmatics*, I, 1, 55.

5. William H. Willimon, ed., *Sermons from Duke Chapel: Voices from "A Great Towering Church"* (Durham, NC: Duke University Press, 2005).

6. As a side note: Greater than the fear of long sermons is the anxiety that a sermon fails to say anything that can't be heard more conveniently elsewhere.

7. Aristotle ideas, per Richard Lischer, ed., *The Company of Preachers: Wisdom in Preaching* (Grand Rapids, MI: Eerdmans, 2002), 355–58.

8. Gregory the Great, *The Pastoral Rule*, in Lischer, *Company of Preachers*, 355–58.

9. Karl Barth, *The Preaching of the Gospel*, trans. B. E. Hooke (Philadelphia: Westminster Press, 1963), 74.

10. Ronald J. Allen, *Hearing the Sermon: Relationship, Content, Feeling* (Channels of Listening; St. Louis: Chalice, 2004). Allen gives a rationale and suggests ways for preachers to listen to their listeners, respecting the rich diversity of how different people hear. See also David J. Schlafer, *Surviving the Sermon: A Guide to Preaching for Those Who Have to Listen* (Cambridge, MA: Cowley, 1992); Roger E. Van Harn, *Pew Rights: For People Who Listen to Sermons* (Grand Rapids, MI: Eerdmans, 1992).

11. Fred B. Craddock, *As One without Authority*, rev. ed. (St. Louis: Chalice, 2001).

12. Fred B. Craddock, *Preaching* (Nashville: Abingdon, 1985), 183.

13. Fred B. Craddock, *Overhearing the Gospel*, rev. ed. (St. Louis: Chalice, 2002), 120.

14. Craddock, *Preaching*, 183.

15. Leonora Tubbs Tisdale, *Preaching as Local Theology and Folk Art*, Fortress Resources for Preaching (Minneapolis: Fortress, 1997).

16. David Buttrick, *Homiletic: Moves and Structures* (Philadelphia: Fortress, 1987); see especially part 2.

17. Joseph R. Jeter Jr. and Ronald J. Allen, *One Gospel, Many Ears: Preaching for Different Listeners in the Congregation* (St. Louis: Chalice, 2002).

18. Henry H. Mitchell, *The Recovery of Preaching* (San Francisco: Harper & Row, 1977), 11.

19. Van Der Geest, quoted in Allen, *Hearing the Sermon*, 123–63.

20. Eric Reed, "The Preaching Report Card: Today's Listeners Grade Pastors on What They Hear from the Pulpit," *Leadership* 20 (Summer 1999): 82–84.

21. Lori Carrell, *The Great American Sermon Survey* (Wheaton, IL: Mainstay Church Resources, 2000). The survey questions were open-ended: (1) How much time do you think it takes a preacher to prepare a sermon? (2) How long should the sermon last? Why? (3) Do you think most preachers feel nervous before preaching? (4) What is your inner reaction to most sermons you hear? (5) Why do you listen to sermons? (6) Do you regularly talk to your preacher about their sermons? Yes or No? Why or Why not? (7) Describe something you gained (or learned) from a specific sermon. (8) How are you and your preacher alike? How are you different? (9) Please rank in order the following components of the church service based on "impacts my spiritual life the most": group singing, special music performed by others, prayer, dramatic presentation skits, communion, sermon, testimony or personal sharing, and liturgy. (10) If you could get one message across to all preachers in the United States, what would it be?

22. Carrell, *The Great American Sermon Survey*, 150–54.

23. Carrell, *The Great American Sermon Survey*, 95.

24. The survey and its results are at William H. Willimon, "Lay Response to Preaching," in *Concise Encyclopedia of Preaching*, ed. William H. Willimon and Richard Lischer (Louisville: Westminster John Knox, 1995), 302–4.

25. Contra Lenny Luchetti, *Preaching with Empathy: Crafting Sermons in a Callous Culture* (Nashville: Abingdon, 2018).

26. Bonhoeffer, quoted in Willimon, *Preachers Dare*, 18.

27. I read about this exercise and its interpretation in Mark Allan Powell, *What Do They Hear? Bridging the Gap Between Pulpit and Pew* (Nashville: Abingdon, 2007), 3–5.

28. "God does not always move us when we desire to be moved, and everything that moves us deeply is not God" (Long, *The Witness of Preaching*, 41).

29. Quoted in Barth, *Church Dogmatics*, I, 1, 49.

30. Quoted in Hughes Oliphant Old, *The Reading and Preaching of the Scriptures*, vol. IV, 20 (Grand Rapids, MI: Eerdmans, 2007), 189.

5. Hearers of the Sermon

1. For Fleming Rutledge's sermon, see https://www.youtube.com/watch?v=ugL4Z5jv1Rg.

2. Kate Murphy, *You're Not Listening: What You're Missing and Why It Matters* (New York: Macmillan, Celadon Books, 2019).

3. Murphy, *You're Not Listening*, 89.

4. Murphy, *You're Not Listening*, 173.

5. Will Willimon, *Aging: Growing Old in Church* (Grand Rapids, MI: Baker Academic, 2020), 77–79.

6. Elaine Pagels, *Why Religion? A Personal Story* (New York: HarperCollins, 2018), 2–3.

7. One of the perks of being a pastor is that one hears some kinky, faith-engendering stories that lead you to exclaim, "Can't believe Jesus pulled a stunt like that! Who knew God was so resourceful?"

8. Lischer, *Company of Preachers*, 400.

6. Responding to the Sermon

1. Barth, *Church Dogmatics*, I, 1, 152.
2. Willimon, *Preachers Dare*, 4–5.
3. Barth, *Church Dogmatics*, I, 1, 246.

7. Hearing Aid

1. Though not a biblical sin, boredom, especially when committed by preachers, is an offense against the Holy Spirit, who promises to liven up even the most tedious life or lackluster congregation. Critics said nasty things about Jesus; nobody ever accused him of being dull.

2. I'm indebted to Eugene Lowry for this idea of "trouble"; see *The Homiletical Plot: The Sermon as Narrative Art Form* (Atlanta: John Knox, 1980), 14–16.

3. See William H. Willimon, *Pastor: The Theology and Practice of Ordained Ministry*, rev. ed. (Nashville: Abingdon, 2016), 6.

4. America as mission field was the theme of Stanley M. Hauerwas and William H. Willimon's *Resident Aliens: Life in the Christian Colony*, 25th Anniversary Ed., (Nashville: Abingdon, 2014).

5. Lischer, *Company of Preachers*, 400.

6. Anne Lamott, *Traveling Mercies* (New York: Anchor, Knopf Doubleday, 2000), 87–88.

7. I'm happy for you to talk back to me about this book: will@duke.edu.

8. Here, I've been inspired by Adler and Van Doren, *How to Read a Book*, 54.

9. Will Willimon, *Accidental Preacher: A Memoir* (Grand Rapids, MI: Eerdmans, 2019), 122–23.

10. Willimon, *Accidental Preacher*, 138.

INDEX OF NAMES

INDEX OF SCRIPTURE